MAGNA FAMILY
LIBRARY

VEGETARIAN COOKING MADE EASY

MAGNA FAMILY
LIBRARY

VEGETARIAN COOKING MADE EASY

DEBORAH GRAY

MAGNA
BOOKS

First published in the UK
1990 by Ward Lock
a Cassell Imprint
Villiers House, 41/47 Strand, London, WC2N 5JE

This edition has been produced in 1995 for Magna Books,
Magna Road, Wigston, Leicester, LE18 4ZH, UK

For further information about Magna Books please contact:
Magna Books,
Magna Road, Wigston
Leicester LE18 4ZH, UK

ISBN 1-85422-867-6

Typeset by Columns of Reading Ltd

Printed and bound in Finland

CONTENTS

CONTENTS

INTRODUCTION

Today more and more people are becoming vegetarians, maybe for health reasons, or because of ecological or animal welfare concerns. Even if you and your family fight shy of becoming committed vegetarians, there is a sound argument for including regular vegetarian meals as part of your diet. Many vegetarian meals are quick and easy to prepare, as this book proves. As an added bonus, vegetarian meals tend to be cheaper than meat-based meals – you can buy an awful lot of beans for the price of a steak!

Nutritionalists tell us that in order to improve our general standard of health, we should eat less fat and increase our intake of fibre. A vegetarian diet fulfils these requirements because vegetable protein in the form of beans, pulses and grains has built-in fibre as opposed to the built-in fat found in animal-based proteins. However, protein in the form of eggs, cheese and milk does contain significant quantities of saturated fats (the type of fats that we should eat less of) so plan meals carefully to make sure that a variety of foods are eaten during the course of the day.

True vegetarians cut out all animal meats, poultry and fish although they do eat dairy products, such as eggs, cheese and milk. Some less ardent vegetarians eat fish, but check before planning a meal; if in doubt assume fish is excluded, as we have done in this book.

A more rigid eating regime is followed by vegans, who also exclude all dairy products from their diet.

They may also avoid honey, which they regard as an animal product. If you are expecting a vegan for dinner, it is best to stick to vegetable-based dishes and take care to use only vegetable or nut-based oils and margarines. You can make dishes requiring milk provided you substitute soya milk for cow's milk. Dishes suitable for vegans included in this book are marked with a V.

THE LONE VEGETARIAN

Many families are now faced with the prospect of having one member of the family who will not touch meat and another who refuses to give it up. In such households it is best to be on the look-out for recipes which are easy to adapt to suit both requirements, and this can be done without involving any extra work.

If cooking a traditional roast, choose a vegetable accompaniment that could be eaten as a vegetarian main course. For instance, leeks in cheese sauce would be delicious with roast lamb and roast potatoes (cooked in oil, not lard or dripping), and would go down well with everyone. If you think that the leeks alone are not exciting, remove a good portion for the vegetarian and add some canned butter beans or some cashew nuts for added protein. Always keep cans of beans handy, as they can quickly be added to vegetable dishes to add bulk, colour and interest.

Another solution is to choose dishes to which meat can be added as an optional extra. Make a vegetable stew. Take off the portion for the meat-eater and add to it diced beef or lamb which has been evenly browned in a little hot fat, and continue to cook until tender. The meat-based dish will probably require longer cooking than its vegetarian counterpart. Similarly, if cooking spaghetti Bolognese, divide the mixture in two after softening the onions, add mince to one pan and brown, then add the tomatoes and remaining ingredients to both dishes and call the vegetarian dish 'Neopolitan-style spaghetti'. One thing is for sure – you will soon become a creative cook!

For further information contact: The Vegetarian Society of the U.K., Parkdale, Dunham Road, Altrincham, Cheshire WA14 4QG and the Vegan Society, 33–35 George Street, Oxford OX1 2AY.

FREEZING

Many of the dishes in this book are suitable for freezing, so if you make a dish specially for a vegetarian, do not make tiny quantities, just freeze the remaining portions for another time. As a general rule, cooked vegetable dishes freeze for up to three months, unless highly spiced in which case six weeks is usually the maximum. It is better to slightly undercook vegetables and pasta dishes destined for the freezer as they will finish cooking while being reheated. All dishes suitable for freezing are marked with an F in the text.

MICROWAVE COOKING

All the microwave tips in this book are written for a 650 watt oven. Increase or decrease the suggested times according to the output of your machine. As a general rule, vegetables are excellent cooked in the microwave, but items which require plenty of liquid, such as soups, pasta, and large quantities of vegetables, are often cooked just as quickly on the conventional hob.

SHOPPING TIPS

Vegetarians tend to be health-conscious, preferring

wholefoods to processed foods. Select foods carefully, choosing those which contain the least additives, sugars (including artificial sweeteners), and those with the lowest fat content. Check too that all the fats in a product are vegetable not animal; animal fats are often used in cakes, biscuits, and even in savoury snacks like crisps. Avoid any products containing gelatine as this is obtained from animal carcases.

Organic vegetables, grains and flours are free from chemical pesticides and fungicides, in addition, organic fruit will not be waxed to make it shiny and appetizing. Although more expensive, organic produce tends to have more flavour, and on a global level such farming methods are kinder to the environment.

STOCKS

Many favourite recipes call for beef or chicken stock; in its place you can use vegetable stock. Commercial vegetable stock cubes are now widely available although most are salty, so dishes made with these require less seasoning. Health food shops stock some low-sodium stock cubes or you can buy a jar or tube of vegetable stock paste, which has a more subtle flavour. A simple stock can be made by saving vegetable cooking water; keep a covered bowl in the refrigerator adding the cooled water after draining the vegetables. This stock can be kept for three to four days before use. Otherwise, make your own stock following the recipe on page 17.

BEANS AND PULSES

For the sake of time and convenience, most of the recipes in this book specify canned beans. However, you can cook your own. Most beans need to be soaked for several hours. Alternatively, cover them with water, boil for five minutes and leave to stand for two hours. Once soaked, the beans should be rinsed and covered with clean water and brought to the boil. Let the beans cook rapidly for at least 10 minutes to remove harmful toxins, then reduce heat and let the beans simmer until tender.

To cook beans in the microwave, soak or cover in water and cook on HIGH for eight to ten minutes, until the water boils, then boil for another two minutes. Leave to stand for two hours. The time taken to cook in the microwave is approximately the same as for conventional cooking.

Lentils do not need soaking or brisk boiling. Cooked beans and pulses can be frozen, providing a ready supply for quick-to-prepare meals.

Type	Minutes
Split lentils (no soaking)	20–30
Whole lentils (no soaking)	30–45
Split peas (no soaking)	40–45
Aduki, black-eyed beans, cannellini, flageolets, red kidney beans	45–50
Haricots	50–60
Broad beans, butter or lima beans, pinto beans, chick-peas, whole green peas	60–90
Soya beans	120

IN THE STORECUPBOARD

There are a few basic ingredients from which a quick and simple meal can be made with the addition of very few ingredients. In addition, they occur regularly in the recipes in this book. You will find it useful to have a permanent supply in the storecupboard.

Selection of dried beans
Dried peas
Lentils (red and brown)
Soup mix

Brown rice
Selection of dried pasta
Bulgur wheat

Almonds
Brazil nuts
Cashew nuts
Hazelnuts
Peanuts
Walnuts

Canned tomatoes (various sizes)
Small and large cans of beans (kidney, butter beans, cannellini)
Commercial baked beans
Canned sweetcorn
Canned ratatouille
Ready-made tomato pasta sauce
Soya milk

Tomato purée
Garlic paste
Freshly ground black pepper
Sea salt
Soy sauce
Sunflower oil
Good selection of herbs and spices
Vegetable stock cubes or paste

Mayonnaise
French dressing

IN THE FREEZER

Selection frozen vegetables
Fresh pasta
Chopped fresh herbs

NOTES ON INGREDIENTS

★ **AGAR AGAR**   A gelatine substitute made from seaweed. The final jelly will be slightly cloudy.

★ **CHEESE**   The rennet added to milk in cheese-making is derived from animals; vegetarian rennet is available and cheeses made with it are labelled as vegetarian. A wider selection is available in health food stores. Check on the nature of the vegetarian you are entertaining as most do not object to eating ordinary cheese.

★ **EGGS**   Preferably free-range.

★ **FLOUR**   Most recipes in this book call for wholemeal flour or, for a lighter effect, a combination of white and wholemeal flour. Wholemeal flour is used for its added fibre and for its 'wholefood' value, but there is no harm in using white flour if you prefer.

★ **HERBS**

All herbs are dried except parsley, which is assumed to be fresh throughout. If unavailable substitute 1 × 5 ml spoon/1 tsp of dried herbs for 1 × 15 ml spoon/1 tbsp fresh herbs.

★ **MARGARINE**

On health grounds it is better to use sunflower or soya margarines. These are lower in saturated fats than the hard margarines. Butter may be used but again, it is high in saturated fats.

★ **OILS**

Choose sunflower, corn, or soya oils, which are high in polyunsaturated fats. Bottles labelled 'vegetable oil' are usually high in palm oil, which is high in saturated fat. Olive oil is a monosaturated fat which seems to be neutral or even slightly beneficial to health. Nut oils are good in salad dressings or for adding a little extra flavour to vegetables.

★ **SOYA MILK**

Made from soya beans. This can be used in sauces, custards and milk puddings. It has a slightly thin, chalky flavour which is masked in these dishes, and it does reduce the fat content quite dramatically. Suitable for vegans.

★ **TSP**
(textured
soya protein)

Imitation meat product derived from soya beans. It has not been used in this book but might be useful if feeding a lone vegetarian.

★ **TOFU**

Another derivative from the soya bean, this time in the form of high-protein curd. It can be deep fried or marinated and cooked. It comes in 250 g/8 oz packages from health food shops. Add it to salads, or use it to make low-fat 'cheesecakes'.

★ **YEAST**
EXTRACT

Useful to add to any dish that seems thin in flavour. Season foods with care as it is high in salt.

NOTES ON RECIPES

All spoon measurements are level.
Eggs are size 3 (standard), unless stated otherwise.
Can sizes are given to the nearest whole number.
Use only metric or imperial measurements when making recipes.
Recipes serve 4, unless otherwise stated.
F suitable for freezing.
V suitable for vegans.

BASIC RECIPES

BÉCHAMEL SAUCE

F

40 g/1½ oz butter
40 g/1½ oz plain flour
300 ml/½ pint milk
75 g/3 oz cheese such as Cheddar,
  Gruyere or Parmesan
salt and freshly ground black
  pepper
1 egg yolk (optional)
pinch nutmeg (optional)

Melt the butter in a small pan then stir in the flour and cook over a low heat for 1 minute, stirring constantly. Remove the pan from the heat and gradually stir in the milk. Return the pan to a moderate heat and cook gently, stirring constantly, until the sauce thickens. Stir in the cheese and seasoning to taste.

For a richer sauce, remove the sauce from the heat and allow to cool for a couple of minutes, then stir in the egg yolk and flavour with nutmeg, if desired.

☆ Microwave tip

Melt the butter in a bowl on HIGH for 1 minute, stir in the flour and then slowly add the milk. Cook for 2–4 minutes, stirring every 30 seconds until the sauce thickens. Add the cheese and cook for 1 minute. Stir until melted.

TOMATO SAUCE   FV

2 × 15 ml spoon/2 tbsp olive oil
1 medium onion, chopped
1 small carrot, grated
1–2 cloves of garlic, crushed
*400 g/14 oz can chopped
    tomatoes, drained*
*2 × 15 ml spoon/2 tbsp tomato
    purée*
*50 ml/2 fl oz/¹⁄₄ cup red wine
    (optional)*
1 tsp basil or marjoram
*salt and freshly ground black
    pepper*

Heat the oil in a pan and add the onions and carrot, and cook gently until the onion is soft and clear. Then add the garlic and cook for a further minute. Stir in the remaining ingredients, adding tomato liquids if wine not used; season to taste. Simmer the sauce gently until thickened. Sauce may be left chunky or may be puréed until smooth.

VEGETABLE STOCK   FV

*1 × 15 ml spoon/1 tbsp
    sunflower oil*
1 large onion, chopped
2 sticks celery, chopped
2 carrots, chopped
2 potatoes, chopped
1 small turnip, chopped
1.5 litres/2¹⁄₂ pints water
1 bay leaf
*2 bouquet garni or a few sprigs
    fresh herbs*

Heat the oil in a large pan, add all the vegetables, and soften them over a gentle heat for about 5 minutes, without letting them go brown. Add the water and herbs and bring to the boil, then cover and simmer for 1¹⁄₂–2 hours. Strain and cool. Keeps for 4 days refrigerated, or may be frozen.

★ Tip

For a richer stock, stir in dark soy sauce to taste.

PANCAKES F

These are rich pancakes, perfect for savoury or for sweet fillings. They use a combination of wholemeal and white flours, which makes them lighter than 100% wholemeal pancakes. Make the batter in a food processor or by hand.

50 g/2 oz plain wholemeal flour
50 g/2 oz plain white flour, sifted
  with a good pinch salt
2 eggs
2 × 15 ml spoons/2 tbsp
  sunflower oil
240 ml/8 oz milk
sunflower oil for frying

If you are using a food processor, place all the ingredients in the bowl and blend for 1–2 minutes until smooth.

If making by hand, place the flour in a bowl, make a well in the centre and add the eggs, oil and about one-third of the milk. Beat with a wooden spoon until smooth, add the remaining milk and beat with a balloon whisk for 1–2 minutes until smooth. Leave to stand for 30 minutes.

To fry the pancakes, brush a small frying-pan with oil and heat until very hot, add about 2 × 15 ml spoons/2 tbsp of the batter and tilt the pan so that the surface of the pan is covered with a thin layer or batter. Fry until set and golden, toss or flip the pancake over using a fish slice and cook the second side. Keep hot if using immediately; repeat for remaining pancakes, brushing the pan lightly with oil between each one.

Makes 10–12 pancakes.

SHORTCRUST PASTRY

Some people find wholewheat pastry too heavy, so you may prefer to use half white flour and half wholemeal flour as in the recipe below. A note of caution: traditional pastry recipes use lard, which is unacceptable to vegetarians. Here, white vegetable fat is used and is available in all supermarkets. If you decide to buy ready-made pastry, do check that it does not contain animal fats.

100 g/4 oz wholemeal self-raising flour
100 g/4 oz white self-raising flour sifted with a pinch salt
50 g/2 oz sunflower margarine
50 g/2 oz white vegetable fat
2–3 tbsp cold water

Place the flour in a bowl. Cut the fat into small pieces and rub into the flour using the fingertips until the mixture resembles fine bread-crumbs. Using a palette knife, add sufficient water to bind the pastry together and make a manageable dough. For best results, wrap in greaseproof paper and chill for 30 minutes before use.

<u>Variations</u>

Rich shortcrust pastry Use butter instead of margarine and vegetable fat, and bind together with egg yolk.

Cheese pastry Add a pinch of cayenne pepper and mustard powder to the flour and stir 50–75 g/2–3 oz finely grated cheese into the mixture before binding.

Orange pastry Make shortcrust pastry as above substituting butter for margarine. Add the grated rind of 1 orange to the mixture before binding with orange juice.

SOUPS

Many traditional soups need little adaptation to transform them into perfect vegetarian fare – simply use a Vegetable Stock (page 17). Serve them for lunch with a warm, crusty loaf and a hunk of cheese or as the perfect beginning for an elegant meal.

MINESTRONE   F V

The ultimate hearty soup.

2 × 15 ml spoon/2 tbsp olive oil
1 onion, chopped
1 clove of garlic, crushed
1 stick of celery, chopped
1 carrot, diced
1 medium potato, diced
1 courgette, sliced
¼ head cabbage, shredded
2 × 15 ml/2 tbsp tomato purée
1.2 litres/2 pints vegetable stock
1 bay leaf
½ tsp basil
½ tsp oregano
2 × 15 ml spoon/2 tbsp chopped parsley
salt and freshly ground black pepper
400 g/14 oz can cannellini beans
grated Parmesan cheese, to serve

Heat the oil in a large pan, add the onion and cook for 3 minutes; then add the garlic and cook for 1 minute. Continue adding the vegetables one at a time and cooking for 1 minute until they are all used. Add tomato purée, stock, herbs and seasoning to taste. Bring to the boil, cover and simmer for 40 minutes. Add the beans and cook for a further 15 minutes. Serve garnished with Parmesan cheese (except for vegans).

Serves 6.

CREAM OF ONION SOUP

25 g/1 oz butter or margarine
450 g/1 lb onions, chopped
25 g/1 oz plain flour
½ tsp mustard powder
600 ml/1 pint stock or water
150 ml/¼ pint milk
salt and freshly ground black
 pepper
1 egg yolk, beaten

Melt the butter or margarine in a pan and add the onions. Cook over a gentle heat until the onions are soft and clear. Sprinkle over the flour and mustard and stir into the buttery onions. Gradually add the stock or water allowing the mixture to boil between additions to prevent lumps forming. Season to taste, then simmer for 20 minutes until the onions are very soft. Add the milk and heat through without boiling. Remove from the heat and cool for a few moments, then stir in the egg yolk. Reheat without boiling, stirring constantly until thickened.

TOMATO SOUP   F V

Fresh tomato soup is infinitely more subtle than its canned counterpart.

800 g/1¾ lb ripe tomatoes,
 skinned, deseeded and chopped
225 g/8 oz crusty white bread,
 roughly torn
2 × 5 ml spoons/2 tsp basil
½ × 5 ml spoons/½ tsp sage
3 cloves of garlic, bruised
3 × 15 ml spoons/3 tbsp olive oil
1.2 litres/2 pints vegetable stock
salt and freshly ground black
 pepper

Place the tomatoes in a large pan with the bread, herbs and garlic. Gently heat until the bread disintegrates and the mixture becomes well mixed. Stir in the olive oil, then add the stock and seasoning to taste. Cook the soup gently for about 20 minutes, stirring occasionally, then serve.

CREAM OF CELERY SOUP   F

*1 head of celery, trimmed and
    chopped*
*1 medium red pepper, deseeded
    and chopped*
25 g/1 oz fresh chives, chopped
600 ml/1 pint vegetable stock
150 ml/¼ pint milk
salt and black pepper

Place the celery, pepper and
chives in a pan and pour over the
stock. Bring to the boil, cover and
simmer for 30 minutes until the
celery is soft. Purée in a blender
or press through a sieve. Add milk
and reheat in a clean pan. Season
to taste.

★ Tip

To reduce fat content of creamed soups, use
skimmed or semi-skimmed milk.

CHICK-PEA SOUP   F V

4 × 15 ml spoons/4 tbsp olive oil
2 onions, chopped
2 carrots, thinly sliced
2 cloves of garlic, crushed
1 stick celery, sliced
*2 large tomatoes, skinned and
    sliced*
*2 × 15 ml spoons/2 tbsp tomato
    purée*
*2 × 400 g/14 oz cans chick-peas,
    drained*
1.2 litres/2 pints vegetable stock
*salt and freshly ground black
    pepper*
*2 × 15 ml spoons/2 tbsp lemon
    juice*
*4 × 15 ml spoons/4 tbsp chopped
    parsley*

Heat the oil in a large pan and add
the onions, carrots, garlic and
celery. Cook over a moderate
heat for 5–6 minutes until the
onions begin to brown. Stir in the
tomatoes and tomato purée and
cook for a further 5 minutes. Add
the chick-peas to the pan along
with the stock and seasoning.
Bring to the boil and simmer for
15 minutes.

Purée the soup in a blender and
reheat in a clean pan. Adjust the
seasoning and stir in the lemon
juice and parsley.

PASTA AND BEAN SOUP   F V

2 × 15 m spoons/2 tbsp olive oil
1 onion, chopped
2 cloves of garlic, crushed
200 g/7 oz can tomatoes
1 × 5 ml spoon/1 tsp sage
1.2 litres/2 pints vegetable stock
*200 ml/7 oz can cannellini or
   kidney beans*
*salt and freshly ground black
   pepper*
*150 g/5 oz soup pasta shells
   (conchigliette)*
grated Parmesan cheese

Heat the oil in a pan and fry the onion until soft and clear. Add the garlic and fry for a further minute. Add the tomatoes, sage and stock. Purée half the beans in a blender or pass through a sieve, then add to the soup. Season with salt and pepper. Cover and simmer the soup for 20 minutes.

Add the pasta and cook for a further 10 minutes, or until the pasta is tender. Serve sprinkled with Parmesan cheese (omit for vegans).

★ Tip

As an alternative thickener for this soup, add a little mashed potato and stir into the hot soup. All the beans can then be added whole.

Variation

Curried lentil soup Add 2–3 5 ml spoons/2–3 tsp curry powder and a generous pinch of ground cumin and coriander to the soup with the garlic. Garnish with desiccated coconut.

☆ Microwave tip

The microwave takes quite a long time to heat bulky liquids so the time saved by making soups this way is minimal.

STORECUPBOARD CORN CHOWDER   F

This is a substantial soup, rich and delicious.

25 g/1 oz margarine
1 onion, chopped
2 sticks of celery, chopped
25 g/1 oz plain flour
410 ml/15 oz can evaporated milk
600 ml/1 pint vegetable stock
350 g/12 oz can sweetcorn
420 g/15 oz can potatoes, roughly chopped
100 g/4 oz Cheddar cheese, grated
1 × 5 ml spoon/1 tsp paprika
2 × 5 ml spoons/2 tsp dried parsley
salt and black pepper

Melt the margarine in a large pan and fry the onion and celery until the onion is soft and clear. Sprinkle over the flour and then stir into the vegetables and cook for 1 minute. Slowly add the evaporated milk and stock, allowing the mixture to boil between additions to prevent lumps from forming. Cover and simmer for 5 minutes. Add the remaining ingredients and heat through until the cheese has melted and the potatoes are hot.

ALMOND, POTATO AND WATERCRESS SOUP   F

This elegant soup can be served to the very best company.

3 bunches watercress, washed, thick stalks removed
2 medium potatoes, roughly chopped
25 g/1 oz ground almonds
1 litre/1¾ pints vegetable stock
juice of ½ lemon
generous pinch ground nutmeg
salt
300 ml/½ pint single cream

Reserve a few watercress leaves for garnishing. Place watercress, potatoes, ground almonds and stock in a pan, bring to the boil, cover and simmer until the potatoes are tender. Purée the soup in a blender. Return the soup to a clean pan and add the lemon juice, nutmeg and salt to taste. Stir in the cream and reheat the soup without boiling. Serve garnished with reserved watercress.

Finally, here are recipes for two cold soups that are delicious on hot days and require no cooking.

GAZPACHO   V

200 g/7 oz can tomatoes
540 ml/19 fl oz can tomato juice
1 × 15 ml spoon/1 tbsp tomato
  purée
2 × 15 ml spoons/2 tbsp cider
  vinegar
1 × 5 ml spoon/1 tsp
  Worcestershire sauce
salt and freshly ground black
  pepper
1/4 cucumber, finely diced
1 green pepper, finely chopped
3 spring onions, finely sliced
2 × 15 ml spoons/2 tbsp chopped
  parsley
2 × 15 ml spoons/2 tbsp fresh
  snipped chives

Press the tomatoes through a sieve, then combine with all the remaining ingredients except the herbs. Chill for at least one hour, then stir in the herbs and serve.

COLD CUCUMBER SOUP

50 g/2 oz raisins
150 ml/1/4 pint warm water
450 ml/3/4 pint natural yoghurt
150 ml/1/4 pint milk
1 cucumber, diced
1 hard-boiled egg, finely chopped
4 spring onions, finely sliced
salt and freshly ground black
  pepper
fresh parsley, chives or dill to
  garnish

Soak the raisins in the warm water, then discard the liquid. Mix together the raisins, yoghurt, milk, cucumber, egg and spring onions, and season to taste with salt and pepper. Chill for at least 1 hour before serving, garnished with the fresh herbs.

STARTERS

A starter should be small, tasty and appetizing without being filling. Many starters are based on fresh fruit or vegetables, so there is no shortage of ideas for feeding the vegetarian. Many of the salads found later in the book would also make excellent starters and are often very quick and easy to prepare.

If you are feeding a mixture of vegetarians and non-vegetarians, it is quite appropriate to select a starter which everyone can eat without adaptation.

The selection of crûdités and dips given in this chapter could double as cocktail snacks served with crisps or similar snacks.

MELON WITH WHITE WINE   F V

Cantaloupe melons are fragrant and succulent. If unavailable, any other melon could be substituted.

2 cantaloupe melons
300 ml/½ pint dry white wine
2 × 15 ml spoons/2 tbsp Marsala
sprigs of mint to garnish

Cut the melons in half and remove the seeds. Make melon balls using a melon ball scoop, or cut the flesh into even-sized chunks. Place the melon balls in individual bowls and pour over equal amounts of wine and Marsala. Leave to chill and marinate for at least 1 hour before serving, garnished with sprigs of fresh mint.

★ Tip

Melon balls may be frozen in their marinade, but as they lose their crispy texture slightly upon defrosting, serve still slightly frozen.

CITRUS COCKTAIL   V

This recipe can double as a finale served as a dessert salad with a bowl of Greek-style yoghurt.

1 small grapefruit, divided into segments
1 small pink grapefruit, divided into segments
1 large orange, divided into segments
50 ml/2 fl oz orange juice
2 × 15 ml spoons/2 tbsp orange-flavoured liqueur
1–2 × 15 ml spoons/1–2 tbsp clear honey (optional)
2 × 15 ml spoons/2 tbsp chopped fresh mint

Arrange the fruit in small bowls or on small plates. Squeeze any fruit juices that remain on the pith into a small bowl and add the orange juice and orange-flavoured liqueur. Sweeten to taste with honey, if desired (not for vegans). Pour the juice over the fruit. Chill before serving, sprinkled with chopped mint.

★ Tip

To segment the fruit, remove the skin and visible pith, then take a very sharp knife and, holding the fruit in the palm of the hand, cut either side of the dividing membrane to release the fruit.

CRÛDITÉS WITH DIPS

Choose a selection of vegetables from the following list:

1 small cauliflower, broken into florets
1 green pepper, deseeded and cut
   into thin sticks
1 red pepper, deseeded and cut into
   thin sticks
3 sticks of celery, cut into thin sticks
¼ cucumber, cut into thin sticks
3 carrots, cut into thin sticks
2 red-skinned apples, cored, sliced
   and dipped in lemon juice

Choose one or more of the following dips to accompany
the crûdités.

AVOCADO AND BLUE CHEESE DIP

100 g/4 oz Danish blue cheese,
   crumbled
100 ml/4 fl oz sour cream
2 avocados, peeled and stoned
1 × 15 ml spoon/1 tbsp lemon
   juice
black pepper

Blend the cheese into the sour
cream. Mash the avocado flesh
with the lemon juice, then beat
into the cheese mixture. Season
to taste with black pepper.

CURRY DIP

225 g/8 oz cottage cheese, sieved
2 × 15 ml spoons/2 tbsp natural
  yoghurt
1 × 5 ml spoons/1 tsp curry
  powder
10 cm/4 inches cucumber, peeled
  and grated
1 medium carrot, grated
salt

Beat together the cheese, yoghurt and curry powder. Stir in the cucumber and carrot and season to taste with salt.

CHEATS ONION DIP

1 packet onion soup mix
300 ml/½ pint sour cream

Stir the dry onion soup mix into the sour cream and serve.

WALNUT AND GARLIC DIP

175 ml/6 fl oz mayonnaise
175 ml/6 fl oz double
  cream, whipped
1–2 cloves of garlic, crushed with
  a little salt
50 g/2 oz walnuts, finely ground
1 × 5 ml spoon/1 tsp lemon juice
white pepper

Fold the mayonnaise into the whipped cream then stir in the garlic, walnuts and lemon juice. Add a generous amount of white pepper, to taste.

★ Tip

Make the crûdités earlier in the day, sprinkle with a little water and place in a plastic bag. Blow the bag up like a balloon and tie a knot. Place in the refrigerator. This method is also good for keeping herbs fresh.

AUBERGINE CAVIAR   V

Most Mediterranean countries have a variation on this
delicacy. It looks great served in a mound on a bed of
lettuce and criss-crossed with strips of red pepper. Serve
with a bowl of black olives and pieces of warm pitta
bread or crusty Italian bread.

450 g/1 lb aubergine(s), washed
1 small onion, peeled and
  chopped
1 clove of garlic, crushed
1 large ripe tomato, skinned and
  chopped
4 × 15 ml spoons/4 tbsp olive oil
2 × 5 ml spoons/2 tsp lemon
  juice
1 × 5 ml spoon/1 tsp oregano
salt and freshly ground black
  pepper
red pepper slices to garnish

Pre-heat the oven to 180°C/350°F/
gas 4. Place the aubergine(s) in
the oven and cook, turning frequently until the skins are black
and wrinkled and the flesh feels
very soft. Leave until cool enough
to handle. Remove the skins,
halve the aubergines, scoop out
the seeds and discard, and chop
the flesh.

Mix together all the ingredients
and purée in a blender in two
batches. Adjust the seasoning,
cover the surface with cling film
to prevent a skin from forming,
and chill. Serve garnished with
thin slices of red pepper.

MUSHROOM PÂTÉ

This pâté is rich and full of flavour. It is delicious served
with warm, wholewheat toast triangles or melba toast.
It should be made a day in advance.

25 g/1 oz soft margarine
4 spring onions, chopped
2 cloves of garlic, crushed
225 g/8 oz field mushrooms,
  chopped
125 g/5 oz curd cheese

Melt the margarine in a pan and
cook the onion and garlic until
soft. Stir in the mushrooms and
cook for about 10 minutes until
soft. Transfer the vegetables to
the blender using a slotted spoon.

40 g/1½ oz medium oatmeal or
   wholewheat breadcrumbs
1 × 5 ml spoon/1 tsp soy sauce
1 × 15 ml spoon/1 tbsp port or
   sherry
salt and freshly ground black
   pepper
2 × 15 ml spoons/2 tbsp chopped
   parsley
2 button mushrooms, to garnish

Add the cheese, oatmeal or breadcrumbs, soy sauce and port or
sherry, and purée until smooth.
Alternatively, press the vegetables
through a sieve and beat in the
remaining ingredients. Season to
taste and stir in the parsley.

Divide between 4 individual
ramekin dishes and cover the top
of the pâté with cling film, then
chill overnight. Garnish with
slices of button mushroom before
serving.

MUSHROOMS À LA GRECQUE

A versatile dish that can be served hot or cold with toast
fingers.

450 g/1 lb bottom mushrooms,
   sliced

Marinade
juice of 1 lemon
150 ml/¼ pint tomato juice
1 onion, finely chopped
1 clove of garlic, crushed
1 × 15 ml spoon/1 tbsp chopped
   parsley
2.5 ml/½ tsp celery salt
2.5 ml/½ tsp thyme
2.5 ml/½ tsp coriander seeds
freshly ground black pepper
fresh parsley, to garnish

Combine all the ingredients for
the marinade and leave to stand
for 30 minutes to allow the
flavours to blend.

Place the mushrooms in a
casserole dish and pour over the
marinade. Cook in the oven for
25 minutes until the mushrooms
are soft. Serve hot or cold.

POTTED STILTON CHEESE

75 g/3 oz *unsalted butter,*
  softened
275 g/10 oz *Stilton cheese*
2 × 15 ml *spoons/2 tbsp port*
50 g/2 oz *walnuts, roughly cut*
¼ tsp *cayenne pepper*
lemon slices, to garnish
crackers, celery sticks to serve

Mix two-thirds of the butter into the Stilton cheese using a small wooden spoon. Mix in the port, nuts and cayenne pepper. Pack the mixture into a single terrine or individual ramekin dishes. Melt the remaining butter, strain through a clean tea-strainer and pour over the potted cheese to seal. Allow to cool. Garnish with lemon slices. Do not serve chilled.

Variation

Stilton celery sticks Omit the final 25 g/1 oz butter and use the potted cheese to fill celery sticks for buffet 'finger food'.

□ Hint

The cheese is much easier to mix in if it has been left to sit at room temperature for a couple of hours before beginning to prepare this dish.

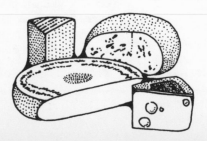

SWISS-STYLE BAKED EGGS

This dish is a classic, as is its variation. Be sure that you use really good fresh eggs.

25 g/1 oz butter, melted
4 eggs
salt and freshly ground black pepper
75 g/3 oz Gruyère cheese, thinly sliced
4 × 15 ml spoons/4 tbsp dry white wine

Pre-heat the oven to 200°C/400°F/gas 6.

Divide the butter between 4 ramekin dishes, then carefully break an egg into each dish. Season with salt and pepper and top with cheese. Pour 1 × 15 ml spoon/1 tbsp of wine over each dish, and bake for 5 minutes until the cheese has melted and the eggs are set. Serve immediately.

Variation

Creamy baked eggs Substitute single cream for the wine and sprinkle a pinch of nutmeg over each egg before baking.

★ Tip

You could add a small slice of prosciutto (Italian-style raw ham) or ordinary cooked ham on top of the eggs for meat-eaters.

☆ Microwave tip

Before adding the cheese, pierce the egg yolks three times with a cocktail stick, then bake the eggs for 4–5 minutes on HIGH until set, turning each dish through 180° once. Add the cheese and cook for 1–2 minutes on LOW until the cheese has melted.

SNACKS AND LIGHT DISHES

Whether for a light lunch, a quick tea-time bite or a late evening filler, you'll find these vegetarian recipes extremely useful.

VEGETABLE BURGERS   F V

These burgers have a little curry powder added to the ingredients to give them a rich and full flavour. They can be served in a burger bun with the same toppings as used for a meat-based burger.

350 g/12 oz cooked potatoes, mashed
350 g/12 oz cooked parsnip or swede, mashed
25 g/1 oz margarine
1 onion, finely chopped
1 clove of garlic, crushed
½–2 × 5 ml spoon/½–2 tsp curry powder, to taste
4 × 15 ml spoons/4 tbsp milk or soya milk
1 × 15 ml spoon/1 tbsp chopped parsley
50 g/2 oz chopped almonds
50 g/2 oz rolled porridge oats
salt and freshly ground black pepper
2 × 15 ml spoons/2 tbsp wholewheat plain flour

Pre-heat the oven to 190°C/350°F/gas 5.

Melt the margarine and cook the onions until soft and clear, add the garlic and curry powder and add for a further minute. Beat the onion mixture into the mashed vegetables along with the milk, then stir in the parsley, almonds and oats. Season to taste with salt and pepper.

Divide the mixture into 8 equal-sized pieces and shape into burgers. Roll the burgers in the flour and then place on a greased baking sheet to cook. Place in the oven for 25 minutes until brown.

★ Tip

These burgers can be adapted for meat-eaters by omitting the milk, potatoes and parsnip or swede, adding instead 450 g/1 lb mince to the softened onion mixture and cooking until evenly browned; drain off fat. Add the remaining ingredients using sufficient beaten egg to bind. These burgers have a good, crunchy texture.

LATKES

F

These potato rissoles are served in America for brunch with sour cream and apple purée – it's a far more delicious combination than it sounds!

450 g/1 lb potatoes, peeled and grated
1 small onion, grated
2 eggs, beaten
2 × 15 ml spoons/2 tbsp plain flour
salt and pepper
vegetable oil for shallow frying

Place the grated vegetables between several sheets of absorbent paper and press to absorb the excess liquid. In a bowl, combine the vegetables, eggs, flour and seasoning to taste. Mix well.

Heat a little oil in a frying pan and gently drop in the mixture by the spoonful. Fry slowly for about 5 minutes each side until golden-brown on both sides. Drain on absorbent paper and keep warm while frying the remaining latkes.

CHEESE AND FILO TRIANGLES

Filo pastry is available in large supermarkets, delicatessens and Greek food shops. It is a very thin pastry that is layered with melted butter to form the crispest, lightest pastry imaginable. It freezes well, so have a packet on hand.

100 g/4 oz ricotta or cottage cheese
150 g/6 oz feta or Caerphilly cheese
50 g/2 oz Parmesan cheese, grated
2 small eggs, lightly beaten
2 × 15 ml spoons/2 tbsp chopped parsley
pinch grated nutmeg
freshly ground black pepper
about 40 g/1½ oz butter, melted
225 g/8 oz filo pastry

Pre-heat oven to 190°C/350° F/ gas 5.

Put all the cheeses in a bowl and mash them together with a fork (if using Caerphilly, roughly grate first). Beat in the eggs, parsley, nutmeg and pepper.

Brush the bottom of a 20 cm/ 8 inch square baking tin with melted butter. Cut the filo pastry to fit. Place a sheet of pastry in the tin. Brush with melted butter and top with another sheet of pastry, repeat until 8 sheets have been used in total. Spoon the cheese filling over the pastry then layer another 6 sheets of pastry and butter over the top. Brush the top sheet generously with butter. Using a sharp knife, cut 8 triangles through the top layer of pastry. Sprinkle a little water over the top to prevent curling.

Bake for 40 minutes until golden-brown. Serve warm or cold with salads.

PAKORAS V

Indian-style vegetable fritters made from chick-pea flour, which is available from health food and Indian grocers.

100 g/4 oz cauliflower, separated in small florets
1 onion, finely chopped
100 g/4 oz potato, diced
1 green pepper, cut into small dice
450 g/1 lb gram flour (chick-pea flour)
1 × 5 ml spoon/1 tsp chilli powder
1 × 5 ml spoon/1 tsp ground turmeric
1 × 5 ml spoon/1 tsp whole coriander seeds
pinch of bicarbonate of soda
450 ml/3/4 pint water
vegetable oil for deep frying

Prepare the vegetables and set aside. Combine the flour, chilli powder, turmeric, coriander seeds and soda. Mix in the vegetables. Make a well in the centre of the mixture and gradually pour in the water. Mix with hands or wooden spoon until a soft dough is formed.

Heat the oil in a deep pan and gently drop spoonfuls of the mixture into the oil. Cook until crisp and golden-brown. Remove wth a perforated spoon and drain on absorbent paper. Keep hot until all the pakoras are cooked. Serve with mango or coriander chutney.

Variation

Aubergine pakoras Substitute peeled and chopped aubergine for the cauliflower. Sprinkle aubergine liberally with salt and leave for 30 minutes, rinse and pat dry, then use as cauliflower above.

SOUFFLÉ POTATOES

4 large old potatoes, scrubbed
oil for brushing

Filling
50 g/2 oz Cheddar cheese, grated
2 small eggs, separated
25 g/1 oz butter or margarine
1 × 15 ml spoon/1 tbsp chopped
  parsley
salt and pepper

Pre-heat the oven to 200°C/400°F/gas 6.

Brush the skins of the potatoes all over with oil and bake for about 1 hour, until soft. Cut the top off each potato and carefully remove the flesh, leaving the skins intact.

Mash the potato in a bowl and beat in the cheese, egg yolk, butter and parsley. Season to taste with salt and pepper. Whisk the egg whites until stiff and fold into the potato mixture, return to the potato skins, piling the mixture up on top. Return to the oven for about 20 minutes until the filling is golden, and serve piping hot.

☆ Microwave tip

Cook the potatoes for 10–12 minutes on HIGH until tender. Reheat filled potatoes for 6–8 minutes until the filling feels firm.

★ Tip

For simple toppings to go on baked potatoes look at the dip recipes (pages 28–29).

NACHOS

A tasty snack from Mexico. It's great served with drinks but do make plenty!

1 package spicy tortilla chips
*2 tomatoes, skinned and
 chopped*
*100 g/4 oz Double Gloucester
 cheese*
*2 × 15 ml spoons/2 tbsp
 chilli sauce*

Pre-heat the oven to 160°C/325°F/ gas 3.

Arrange half of the tortilla chips on an ovenproof dish, sprinkle over half of the tomatoes and cheese; repeat with the remaining chips, tomatoes and cheese. Drizzle the chilli sauce over the top and bake for 10 minutes, until the cheese has melted. Serve hot.

CARROT AND COURGETTE PANCAKES   F

125 g/5 oz carrots
125 g/5 oz courgettes, grated
2 eggs, beaten
*40 g/1½ oz wholemeal or plain
 flour*
¼ tsp bicarbonate of soda
pinch salt
*2 × 15 ml spoons/2 tbsp
 sunflower oil*
*1 quantity Tomato Sauce
 (page 17), (optional)*

Cook the carrots whole in boiling water for about 10 minutes, until not quite cooked. Drain and allow to cool, then grate and combine with the courgettes. Stir together the eggs, flour, bicarbonate of soda and salt, and fold the courgettes and carrots into this mixture.

Heat about one-quarter of the oil in a small skillet or frying-pan and add one-quarter of the batter, flatten into a fat pancake shape and cook over a moderate heat until small bubbles appear on the top of the pancake. Turn the pancake over and cook the second side. Remove from the pan and keep warm; repeat with remaining pancakes. Serve with tomato sauce.

SANDWICH FILLERS

If you are picnicing or packing a lunch for a vegetarian, you may wish to serve something other than a cheese and pickle sandwich. Aubergine Caviar (page 30) and Mushroom Pâté (page 30) are also good sandwich fillers; add a slice of lettuce and a few slices of cucumber for added crunch. The quantities given are sufficient to fill 4 wholemeal baps.

CURRIED FRUIT SANDWICH FILLER

175 g/6 oz low-fat cream cheese
2 × 15 ml spoons/2 tbsp milk
¼–½ × 5 ml spoon/¼–½ tsp curry powder or paste
2 × 15 ml spoons/2 tbsp mango chutney
½ eating apple, finely chopped
1 small banana, sliced
1 × 15 ml spoon/1 tbsp chopped walnuts

Beat together the cream cheese, milk, curry powder or paste and chutney. Fold in the fruit and the walnuts.

HERBY BEAN SPREAD

A slice of tomato goes well on sandwiches made with this spread. It is also good on crackers.

400 g/14 oz can butter beans, drained
25 g/1 oz butter or margarine
1 small clove of garlic, crushed
2 × 15 ml spoons/2 tbsp fresh herbs: parsley , mint, dill, chives, tarragon
few drops lemon juice
salt and freshly ground black pepper

Slip the skins from the butter beans and mash the beans to a paste with the butter or margarine. Mix in the garlic, herbs and lemon juice, salt and pepper to taste.

AVOCADO AND TOMATO FILLER

*1 ripe avocado, peeled and stone
   removed
1 hard-boiled egg, finely chopped
125 g/5 oz low-fat soft cheese
1 × 5 ml spoon/1 tsp lemon juice
salt and freshly ground black
   pepper
few drops Tabasco (optional)
2 ripe tomatoes*

Mash the avocado flesh with the egg, cheese and lemon juice until smooth. Season to taste and add Tabasco, if using. Use as a filler topped with slices of tomato.

PEANUT BUTTER FILLER

*6 × 15 ml spoons/6 tbsp crunchy
   peanut butter
1 carrot, grated
2 × 15 ml spoons/2 tbsp raisins
2 × 15 ml spoons/2 tbsp
   sunflower seeds*

Mix all the ingredients together and use in sandwiches or baps or even on toast.

★ Tip

Peanut butter goes with quite a variety of foods. Try substituting banana, chopped apple or crushed pineapple for the carrot. Alternatively, you could make the American favourite, PBJ – peanut butter and jam – it is best with cherry or strawberry jam. If you prefer it with savoury foods, mix with chopped egg.

MUSHROOM PIZZA F

This short-cut variation on the pizza uses a scone base which dramatically reduces the preparation time.

225 g/8 oz self-raising wholemeal flour (or half wholemeal and half white self-raising flour)
50 g/2 oz margarine
2 × 5 ml spoons/2 tsp mixed herbs
1 egg, lightly beaten
2–4 × 15 ml spoons/2–4 tbsp milk

Topping
2.5 × 15 ml spoons/2½ tbsp sunflower oil
1 onion, cut into rings
1 small clove garlic, crushed
100 g/4 oz mushrooms, sliced
2 × 15 ml spoons/2 tbsp tomato purée
400 g/14 oz can chopped tomatoes, drained
2.5 ml/½ tsp basil
2.5 ml/½ tsp marjoram
salt and freshly ground black pepper
175 g/6 oz Mozzarella cheese, diced, or Cheddar cheese, grated

Pre-heat the oven to 220°C/425°F/gas 7.

To make the base, place the flour in a bowl and rub in the margarine. Stir in the herbs then bind together with the egg and sufficient milk to make a soft but firm dough. Roll out on a floured board to a thickness of about 5 mm/¼ inch. Place on a greased 25 cm/10 inch pizza or pie plate.

For the topping, heat 2 × 15 ml spoons/2 tbsp oil in a frying-pan, add the onion and fry gently for 4 minutes, add the garlic and mushrooms and continue to cook until the mushrooms are tender. Remove the vegetables from the pan and drain on absorbent paper.

Spread the tomato purée over the base, leaving a small edge of base showing all the way around. Top the base with the tomatoes, herbs, salt and pepper, then the onion and mushroom mixture. Finally, sprinkle the cheese on top. Brush the outer rim of the pizza with the remaining oil and bake for 15–20 minutes, until the cheese is bubbling and the outer rim of the base is crisp.

Variations

Pepper pizza In place of mushrooms use half a green and half red pepper, with or without olives.

Popeye pizza Omit mushrooms and replace with 225 g/8 oz lightly cooked spinach mixed with pine kernels and raisins.

★ Tip

Some supermarkets sell pizza bases ready made. They freeze well and make a great standby. Use from frozen and top with one of the suggestions above.

30-MINUTE FAMILY MEALS

These quick and easy main dishes can all be prepared and cooked in under 30 minutes. Some of the dishes in this section are extremely versatile with so many variations that only a few ideas can be given here – you will certainly be able to invent many more to suit your own family's needs and tastes.

LEEKS IN CHEESE SAUCE   F

This is one of the most basic and best-loved vegetable dishes. It can be served as a vegetable side dish with Sunday lunch, or with chops or sausages during the week. Eaten in larger quantities, it doubles as a perfectly adequate vegetarian main course, but the variations below are bound to tempt you.

6 thin leeks, outer leaves removed and cleaned
300 ml/½ pint milk
150 ml/¼ pint water
salt
1 quantity Béchamel sauce flavoured with nutmeg (page 16)
2 × 15 ml spoons/2 tbsp dried breadcrumbs
1 × 15 ml spoons/1 tbsp grated Parmesan cheese

Cut the leeks into thumb-sized pieces and place in a pan with the milk and water and a little salt to taste. Cover and simmer, stirring occasionally, until the leeks are tender, about 5–15 minutes depending on the freshness of the leeks. Drain the leeks and save the liquid. Keep the leeks warm. Use 300 ml/½ pint of the cooking liquid to make the Béchamel sauce (the plain or rich sauce may be used).

Place the leeks in a heatproof dish and pour over the sauce. Mix together the breadcrumbs and Parmesan cheese and sprinkle over the top. Brown under a hot grill.

Variations

Cauliflower cheese Cook the cauliflower in water until tender, drain and continue as above.

Fennel in cheese sauce As for cauliflower cheese.

Broccoli in cheese sauce As for cauliflower cheese.

Celery in cheese sauce As for cauliflower cheese. Alternatively, braise celery in vegetable stock in a moderate oven until tender, drain and proceed as above.

Leek rolls Leave leeks whole and proceed as above. Wrap leeks in ham for non-vegetarians and bake for 30 minutes in a moderate oven.

Leeks in blue cheese Substitute Danish blue, Gorgonzola or Stilton cheese when making the sauce. Do be careful not to over-salt.

Vegetable cheese surprise Make any of the vegetable cheese dishes, but add one or two of the suggestions below before pouring over the sauce. Bake for 30 minutes in a moderate oven, or in the microwave for 10–12 minutes on HIGH.

Add one or two of the following:
4 quartered tomatoes
3 chopped spring onions
50 g/2 oz cashew nuts
50 g/2 oz walnuts
400 g/14 oz can butter beans
400 g/14 oz can brown beans
2 × 15 ml spoons/2 tbsp parsley

☆ Microwave tip

Any of the vegetables mentioned may be cooked in the microwave in 4 tbsp water for approximately 7–9 minutes on HIGH. Follow manufacturer's guidelines for precise timings. The sauce may be cooked in the microwave (page 16), but the topping needs to be grilled as it will be soggy if cooked in the microwave.

STIR-FRIED VEGETABLES WITH SMOKED TOFU   V

Tofu is made from pressed soya bean curd and is very high in protein. Smoked tofu has more flavour than regular tofu and is available from health food stores. This dish may be served as part of a Chinese meal or as a main dish on its own, with noodles or rice.

2 × 15 ml spoons/2 tbsp
vegetable or peanut oil
1 × 5 ml spoon/1 tsp grated root
ginger

Mix together all the ingredients for the sauce.

Heat the oil in a wok or large frying pan and fry the ginger for

225 g/8 oz smoked tofu, cut into 1 cm/½ inch cubes
175 g/6 oz Chinese leaves, shredded
4 spring onions, finely sliced
100 g/4 oz beansprouts
100 g/4 oz mushrooms, sliced
½ red pepper, deseeded and sliced

Sauce
2 × 15 ml spoons/2 tbsp dark soy sauce
2 × 15 ml spoons/2 tbsp red vinegar
1 × 15 ml spoons/1 tbsp sugar
2 × 15 ml spoons/2 tbsp water
2 × 5 ml spoon/2 tsp cornflour

1 minute. Add the tofu and stir fry over a gentle heat until it begins to turn brown. Remove to side of wok, or remove from frying pan altogether using a perforated spoon. Add all of the prepared vegetables and stir fry over a high heat for about 3 minutes, keeping the vegetables moving all the time. Pour over the sauce, return the tofu to the pan, and cook until the sauce thickens, stirring constantly.

Variation

Stir-fried vegetables with cashews Omit bean-curd and substitute 100 g/4 oz cashew nuts, fry in the oil as instructed for bean-curd until browned, then remove from the wok and continue as above.

☐ Hints

Vary this dish for non-vegetarians by marinating 2 sliced chicken breasts in a quantity of the sauce for at least 30 minutes. Drain and stir fry separately, and keep warm. Add with the tofu when the vegetables are cooked.

If unable to obtain smoked tofu, use regular tofu and marinate in a quantity of the sauce, omitting water and cornflour, for at least 1 hour. Drain and add cornflour and water to the sauce and cook the tofu as above.

PASTA

Pasta is a godsend for the cook in a hurry and there are numerous vegetarian pasta dishes. The sauces given here would go with any of the pasta types. All of the pasta dishes are excellent with a mixed salad and crusty bread.

SPAGHETTI NEOPOLITANA   F V

300 g/12 oz spaghetti
1 × 15 ml spoons/1 tbsp oil
1 quantity of Tomato Sauce
  (page 17)
grated Parmesan cheese

Cook the spaghetti in plenty of rapidly boiling salted water along with the oil until just tender, 7–12 minutes. Drain thoroughly. Toss in the hot tomato sauce, and sprinkle with Parmesan cheese to taste.

Variations

Spaghetti with tomato and pine kernels Make the spaghetti Neopolitana as above but add 3 × 15 ml spoons/3 tbsp pine kernels to the hot sauce
Tagliatelle with mushrooms Add 12 g/½ oz butter to the oil when making the tomato sauce and add 100 g/4 oz sliced mushrooms once the onions are soft, and cook until tender. Continue to prepare the sauce as directed. Cook the tagliatelle as spaghetti above.
Penne with chillied tomato sauce Add 1 red chilli, deseeded, with the garlic when making the basic tomato sauce. Cook the penne as spaghetti above. A

400 g/14 oz can of chick-peas, drained, is also good in this recipe.

★ Tip

If making spaghetti for non-vegetarians as well, divide the mixture after cooking the garlic, add about 100 g/4 oz per person of minced beef to one batch, and brown. Drain off excess fats. Add the remaining ingredients to the two batches of sauce. The meat sauce will need cooking for at least 30 minutes.

PENNE WITH BÉCHAMEL SAUCE AND PEAS   F

300 g/10 oz penne
1 × 15 ml spoon/1 tbsp oil
100 g/4 oz frozen peas
1 quantity rich Béchamel sauce
  with Nutmeg (page 16)
grated Parmesan cheese

Bring a pan of salted water to the boil. Add the oil (to stop the pasta sticking together). Drop in the penne and cook rapidly for 5–7 minutes, until the pasta is soft but still a little undercooked. Add the peas and cook for a further 3 minutes until both penne and peas are cooked. Drain thoroughly. Toss in the rich Béchamel sauce and sprinkle with Parmesan cheese to serve.

★ Tip

For non-vegetarians add chopped smoked ham to the sauce.

PASTA SHELLS WITH GORGONZOLA

This is a lovely, rich pasta sauce, perfect for all occasions and incredibly quick to make.

300 g/10 oz pasta shells
(conchiglie)
1 × 15 ml spoon/1 tbsp oil
100 g/4 oz Gorgonzola, at room
temperature
150 ml/¼ pint double cream
salt and freshly ground black
pepper

Cook the pasta shells in plenty of rapidly boiling salted water, to which the oil has been added, until just tender, about 7–12 minutes. Beat together the cheese and cream using a wooden spoon. Place in a double-boiler over the cooking pasta until heated through and amalgamated (a heatproof bowl could be placed directly onto the pan provided the base of the bowl does not touch the water). Season the sauce taking care not to over-salt. Drain the pasta and toss with the sauce.

☆ Microwave tip

Cook the sauce on MEDIUM for 3 minutes, stirring once.

★ Tip

If you are anxious to reduce your fat intake, use a buttermilk-based cream substitute in this dish.

□ <u>Hint</u>

To freeze pasta dishes, undercook the pasta by about 2 minutes. To serve, place in a covered dish in a moderately hot oven until heated through, stir occasionally. Alternatively, cook on HIGH in the microwave for 5 minutes, leave to stand for 2 minutes, stir, then heat for 2 minutes and leave to stand again, stir. Repeat the 2-minute cycle until hot. Reheat pasta dishes that have not been frozen in a double boiler over simmering water or in the microwave on HIGH.

THREE-CHEESE RISOTTO

Wonderful on its own with a crisp salad, or it could be served with ham or sausages for meat-eaters.

25 g/1 oz butter
1 × 15 ml spoon/1 tbsp olive oil
2 cups risotto (arborio) rice
1 onion, finely chopped
900 ml/1½ pints vegetable stock
75 g/3 oz Gruyére cheese, grated
75 g/3 oz Emmenthal cheese, grated
1 × 15 ml spoon/1 tbsp grated Parmesan cheese
salt and freshly ground black pepper

Place butter and oil in a large pan over moderate heat and when the butter has melted, add the rice and onion, fry for 2 minutes, stirring constantly. Pour in the stock and bring to the boil. Cover and simmer for 15–20 minutes until the rice is tender and most of the liquid absorbed. Stir in the cheese and season to taste. Heat through gently until the cheese is hot and melted, and serve immediately. Do not overcook or the cheese will become grainy.

PIPERADE

F

Omit the eggs and you have a delicious vegetable stew called 'peperonata' which is perfect with lamb or with grilled white fish. Served cold it also makes a good salad dish. Piperade is excellent served with warm bread and a mixed bean salad.

2 × 15 ml spoons/2 tbsp olive oil
4 peppers (mixture of green, red and yellow), deseeded and sliced
2 onions, sliced
1 clove of garlic, crushed
4 tomatoes, skinned and sliced
salt and freshly ground black pepper
4 eggs
4 × 15 ml spoons/4 tbsp milk

Heat the oil in a large frying-pan and add the peppers, onions and garlic. Cover the pan and allow vegetables to sweat (soften gently without colouring) over a low heat, stirring occasionally, until the peppers and onion are soft. Add the tomatoes and cook for a couple of minutes, then cover the pan and cook for a further 5 minutes. Season to taste.

Meanwhile, beat together the eggs and milk with a balloon whisk for 2 minutes. Pour into the vegetable mixture and stir with a wooden spoon until the cooked egg has completely blended with the vegetables. Serve immediately.

60-MINUTE FAMILY MEALS

The dishes included in this chapter can be completed within 1 hour. They include nut-based dishes and baked vegetable dishes and flans.

BASIC NUT MIXTURE   V F

Many people equate vegetarian eating with nut roast – but most of those who mock have not tried it. This version is full of taste and texture and it's very filling, so serve it with a light vegetable dish or salad. The basic mixture can be used to make a variety of different dishes, and can often be substituted for minced meat.

25 g/1 oz margarine
1 onion, chopped
1 large carrot
225 g/8 oz mixed nuts: almonds,
   cashews, hazelnuts, peanuts,
   pecans or walnuts
100 g/4 oz wholemeal bread
200 ml/7 fl oz vegetable stock
2 × 5 ml spoons/2 tsp yeast
   extract
1 × 5 ml spoon/1 tsp sage
salt and freshly ground black
   pepper

Melt the margarine in a small pan and cook the onion gently until soft and clear. Meanwhile, grind the carrot, nuts and bread until quite fine in a food processor. Pour the stock and yeast extract into the pan with the onions and stir until the extract has dissolved. Combine with the nut mixture, sage and seasoning.

NUT ROAST   V F

Pre-heat oven to 180°C/350°F/gas 4.

Make one quantity of the basic nut mixture. Press into a greased 500 g/1.1 lb loaf tin. Bake for 30 minutes, until golden-brown. Serve cold or hot with a quantity of Tomato Sauce (page 17) if desired.

★ Tip

You will find that nut loaf slices better chilled.

LAYERED NUT ROAST   F

Prepare as for nut roast above. Spread about 2 × 15 ml spoons/2 tbsp tomato ketchup over the base of the tin, then press in half of the nut mixture. Spread with about 1 × 15 ml spoon/1 tbsp tomato ketchup and then sprinkle 50 g/2 oz Caerphilly cheese over the top. Press the remaining nut mixture into the tin. Bake as for nut roast.

NUT RISSOLES   V F

Make 1 quantity of basic nut mixture. Shape into 6–8 patties and coat in wholemeal breadcrumbs, pressing well into the surface. Shallow fry in hot sunflower oil for about 4 minutes on each side until browned.

VEGETARIAN SHEPHERD'S PIE   F

Pre-heat oven to 200°C/400°F/gas 6. Make 1 quantity basic nut mixture but use 2 carrots and add sufficient stock to make the mixture sloppy. Pour into an ovenproof dish and top with a layer of creamed mashed potatoes. Grate 50 g/2 oz Cheddar cheese over the top and dust with paprika. Bake for about 25 minutes, until the cheese is golden and bubbly.

AUTUMN VEGETABLE COBBLER   V F

300 g/12 oz turnips
300 g/12 oz carrots
300 g/12 oz swede
2 sticks celery, sliced
175 g/6 oz shallots, peeled
2 medium leeks, thickly sliced
2 × 15 ml spoons/2 tbsp oil
*240 ml/8 fl oz vegetable or
    chicken stock*
225 g/8 oz can chopped tomatoes
pinch mixed herbs
*salt and freshly ground black
    pepper*
2 tsp cornflour

Topping
*125 g/4 oz wholemeal plain
    flour*
125 g/4 oz plain flour
2.5 ml/½ tsp salt
*2 × 5 ml spoons/2 tsp baking
    powder*
50 g/2 oz margarine
2.5 ml/½ tsp dried sage
1 tbsp chopped parsley
*50 g/2 oz cheddar cheese,
    finely grated*
150 ml/5 fl oz plain yoghurt
2 × 15 ml spoons/2 tbsp milk

Heat the oven to 190°C/375°F/Gas 5. Peel the turnips, carrots and swede and cut into similar size chunks. Heat the oil in a large frying pan, add all the vegetables and cook over a medium high heat until they begin to brown a little. Turn into a casserole dish, pour over the stock, tomatoes with their juice and season with the herbs, salt and pepper. Cover and cook for 30 minutes in the oven. Blend the cornflour with a 1 × 15 ml spoon/1 tbsp of water, remove the casserole from the oven and stir cornflour into the vegetables. Cover and return to the oven for a further 10 minutes.

Put the flours into a bowl with the salt and baking powder, rub in the margarine. Add the sage, parsley and cheese then mix to a soft dough with the yoghurt and milk. Lightly knead the dough until smooth then roll out to about 1 cm/½ in thick. Using a 5 cm/2 in cutter, cut out rounds. Take the casserole from the oven, increase the temperature to 200°C/400°F/Gas 6. Remove the lid and arrange the rounds of dough, slightly overlapping, on top of the vegetables, brush the tops with a little milk. Cook for a further 20 minutes until the topping is risen and golden.

STUFFED PEPPERS

A Greek-style filling that can be used to stuff all sorts of vegetables. Without the cheese, it also makes a good savoury rice dish to accompany meat dishes.

4 red, green or yellow peppers
4 × 15 ml spoons/4 tbsp olive oil
1 large onion, finely chopped
2 cloves of garlic, crushed
150 g/6 oz cooked long-grain rice
2 tomatoes, skinned and chopped
6 × 15 ml spoons/6 tbsp tomato purée
6 × 15 ml spoons/6 tbsp chopped fresh mint
salt and freshly ground black pepper
50 g/2 oz feta cheese, crumbled, or ricotta or fine cottage cheese
6 × 15 ml spoons/6 tbsp water
1 × 5 ml spoon/1 tsp marjoram

Pre-heat oven to 180°C/350°F/gas 4.

Remove the tops from the peppers and deseed. Blanch in boiling water for 3 minutes then remove and place upside down to drain.

Heat the oil and fry the onion for 4 minutes, add the garlic and continue to cook until the onion is soft and clear. Combine with the rice, tomato, half of the tomato purée, the mint and seasoning to taste. Bring the mixture to the boil and cook for 5 minutes, stirring constantly. Add the cheese, and check the seasoning.

Spoon the filling into the peppers. Mix the remaining tomato purée with the water and marjoram and season lightly. Place peppers tightly packed in a baking dish and pour the sauce around them. Bake for about 30 minutes until the peppers are tender.

Variations

Stuffed tomatoes Omit tomatoes from recipe but use 8 large tomatoes for stuffing. Cut the tops off the tomatoes and remove the flesh, taking care to leave the shells undamaged. Proceed as above, using the tomato flesh in the stuffing.

Stuffed courgettes Cook the courgettes whole in boiling water for 5 minutes. Drain, cool slightly and cut in half lengthwise. Scoop out the flesh leaving the shells intact. Add the courgette flesh to the filling with the rice. Proceed as for stuffed peppers.

☆ <u>Microwave tip</u>

Blanch the peppers in 4 × 15 ml/4 tbsp water on HIGH for 1 minute. Cook the stuffed peppers for 9–12 minutes on HIGH until tender, turning once.

COURGETTE AND MUSHROOM CROUSTADE   F

This is an excellent dish that will impress non-vegetarians.

175 g/6 oz wholemeal breadcrumbs
50 g/2 oz margarine
50 g/2 oz chopped mixed nuts
1 small onion, grated
2 × 15 ml spoons/2 tbsp Parmesan cheese
2 × 15 ml spoons/2 tbsp sunflower seeds
1 × 5 ml spoon/1 tsp sesame seeds
grated rind of ½ lemon

Filling
25 g/1 oz margarine
225 g/8 oz flat mushrooms, sliced
1 large courgette, sliced
450 g/1 lb tomatoes, skinned and sliced
juice of ½ lemon
salt and freshly ground black pepper

Pre-heat the oven to 190°C/375°F/gas 5.

For the croustade, rub the margarine into the breadcrumbs. Mix in the remaining ingredients. Press half of the mixture into a greased ovenproof dish.

To make the filling, melt the margarine in a pan and gently fry the mushrooms and courgettes until tender. Place on top of the croustade base and top with a layer of sliced tomatoes. Sprinkle over the lemon juice and season to taste. Top with remaining croustade mixture and press down firmly. Bake for 30 minutes, until golden.

Variations

Leek croustade Replace filling with 1 quantity Leek in Cheese Sauce (page 44).
Broccoli croustade Omit fried mushrooms and courgettes and replace with 450 g/1 lb steamed broccoli

---

☆ Microwave tip

Cook the completed croustade for 20 minutes on MEDIUM; brown under a hot grill, if desired.

PANCAKES WITH SPINACH AND RICOTTA   F

1 quantity pancakes (page 18)
900 g/2 lb spinach, washed and trimmed
225 g/8 oz ricotta or cottage cheese
salt and freshly ground black pepper
1 quantity Béchamel sauce flavoured with nutmeg (page 16)

Pre-heat the oven to 180°C/350°F/gas 4.

To prepare the filling, cook the spinach with just the water clinging to the leaves for about 5 minutes, until soft but still bright green. Cool slightly, press out all the water and chop. Mix together with the cheese, and seasoning to taste. Divide the filling between the pancakes and roll up. Place in an ovenproof dish and top with Béchamel sauce. Bake for 20 minutes, until the sauce is beginning to brown.

Variation

Pancake stack Pre-heat the oven to 190°C/375°F/gas 5. Make the quantity of pancakes, half of the quantity of spinach and ricotta filling, and 1 quantity of tomato sauce. Lay a pancake on a heatproof plate and top with the spinach filling. Cover with another pancake, and spread that with tomato sauce. Continue layering in this way, ending with a pancake. Grate 50 g/2 oz Cheddar cheese over the top and bake for 20 minutes until the cheese is bubbling. Cut like a cake to serve.

MIXED VEGETABLE CURRY

Don't be put off by the long list of spices, this is not a very hot curry, but the blend of spices gives it an authentic flavour. Serve alone with nan bread.

2 × 15 ml spoons/2 tbsp oil
1 onion, chopped
1 clove of garlic, crushed
1 × 5 ml spoon/1 tsp grated root ginger
1 × 5 ml spoon/1 tsp chilli powder
1 × 5 ml spoon/1 tsp ground coriander
1 × 5 ml spoon/1 tsp ground cumin
1 small cinnamon stick
1 large potato, diced
2 carrots, peeled and diced
300 ml/½ pint vegetable stock
100 g/4 oz French beans
50 g/2 oz okra, left whole
100 g/4 oz frozen peas
200 g/7 oz can tomatoes and juice
salt and freshly ground black pepper

Heat the oil and fry the onions until soft and clear. Add the garlic and spices and fry for 2 minutes, stirring constantly. Add the potato and carrots and fry them in the spices for 1 minute. Add the stock, cover and cook for 10 minutes. Stir in the remaining ingredients, cover and cook until all the vegetables are just tender. Remove the lid and continue cooking until the sauce has thickened.

☆ Microwave tip

Cook the oil and onions on HIGH for 2 minutes, add the garlic and spices and cook for 1 minute. Add the potatoes and carrots, cover and cook for 10 minutes. Add the remaining ingredients using ony 150 ml/¼ pint stock, cover and cook for a further 5 minutes on HIGH or until tender.

BUDGET VEGETABLE HOTPOT

A hearty stew to keep away the winter chills.

2 × 15 ml spoons/2 tbsp
  vegetable oil
1 onion, chopped
2 large carrots, peeled and
  chopped
1 potato, diced
1 small turnip, peeled and diced
1/2 small swede, peeled and diced
1 large parsnip, peeled and
  chopped
2 sticks celery, sliced
2 cloves of garlic, crushed
2.5 cm/1 inch piece root ginger,
  grated
75 g/3 oz pot barley, soaked for
  30 minutes
600 ml/1 pint vegetable stock
1 × 15 ml spoon/1 tbsp tomato
  purée
1 bay leaf
1 × 5 ml spoon/1 tsp mixed
  herbs
salt and freshly ground black
  pepper

Heat the oil in a large pan, add the onion and carrot, and cook gently until the onion is soft and clear. Add all the remaining ingredients and bring to the boil. Cover and simmer, stirring occasionally, for about 20 minutes, until the vegetables are all tender and the barley cooked. Boil rapidly for a few minutes to reduce and thicken the sauce slightly.

★ Tip

If you wish to add meat to a portion of this stew, you will need to brown cubes of beef or lamb in hot fat and then add with the vegetables. You will need to increase the cooking time for the meat stew to a minimum of 45 minutes.

SLOW-COOKING MEALS

The recipes in this chapter are not complicated, but they do take more than an hour to cook and prepare. Many can be made in advance, or can be left to their own devices while you get on with something else.

CHILLI NON CARNI   F V

3 × 15 ml spoons/3 tbsp oil
1 onion, chopped
2 carrots, sliced
1 large green pepper, chopped
1 clove of garlic, crushed
1 × 5 ml spoon/1 tsp cumin
   seeds
½–2 ×5 ml spoons/½–2 tsp
   chilli powder
2 sticks of celery, sliced
4 medium courgettes, sliced
400 g/14 oz can tomatoes
1 × 15 ml spoon/1 tbsp tomato
   purée
1 vegetarian stock cube, dissolved
   in 150 ml/¼ pint water
1 tsp oregano
400 g/14 oz can red kidney
   beans
salt and freshly ground black
   pepper

Heat the oil in a pan and gently fry the onion for 3 minutes, then add the carrots, green pepper and garlic, and continue to cook until the onion is soft and clear. Stir in the cumin seeds and chilli to taste (under-season with chilli as you can add more later). Add the remaining ingredients except for the beans, bring to the boil, cover and cook for 30 minutes. Add the beans and adjust the seasoning to taste, cook for a further 15 minutes.

★ <u>Tip</u>

If you wish to add meat you will need about 100 g/4 oz minced beef per person. Brown the meat in hot fat and drain. Take off required amount of chilli non carni once all the ingredients have been added, and mix in the mince. Do not forget to add beans to both pans of chilli.

☐ <u>Hint</u>

A side dish of sour cream goes well with chilli non carni.

☆ <u>Microwave tip</u>

To microwave, cook the onion, carrots and garlic in the oil in a covered dish for 2 minutes on HIGH, add the remaining ingredients except for the beans, and cook for 12–15 minutes on HIGH, stirring occasionally, until the vegetables are all soft. Add the beans and heat on HIGH for 3 minutes. Leave to stand for 5 minutes.

PASTICHIO F

Traditionally, this dish comprises layers of meat, layers of pasta and a rich cheesy sauce topping. This version uses a well-flavoured lentil mixture that could also be substituted for minced meat in other dishes such as moussaka, shepherd's pie or stuffed marrow. Make a big batch of it and freeze in small quantities to keep on standby.

3 × 15 ml spoons/3 tbsp olive oil
25 g/1 oz butter
1 large onion, chopped
2 cloves of garlic, crushed
1 small green pepper, deseeded and chopped
1 large courgette, diced
100 g/4 oz mushrooms, sliced
225 g/8 oz red lentils, washed and picked over
400 g/14 oz can tomatoes
2 × 15 ml spoons/2 tbsp tomato purée
2.5 ml/½ tsp oregano
2.5 ml/½ tsp ground cinnamon
450 ml/¾ pint vegetable stock
50 ml/2 fl oz red wine (optional)
salt and freshly ground black pepper
200 g/7 oz macaroni (plain or wholemeal)
1 quantity Béchamel sauce (page ??)
2 eggs, well beaten

Pre-heat the oven to 200°C/400°F/ gas 6.

In a large pan, heat together the oil and butter, and gently cook the onion until soft and clear. Add the garlic, green pepper, courgette and mushrooms and cook together for another 5 minutes. Add the lentils, tomatoes, tomato purée, oregano, cinnamon, stock, wine and seasoning to taste. Bring to the boil, cover and simmer for about 45 minutes, until the lentils are soft and most of the liquid has been absorbed.

Meanwhile, cook the macaroni for 10–12 minutes until tender and drain. Place half of the macaroni in a greased ovenproof baking dish and spread over the lentil mixture, then top with the remaining macaroni. Beat the eggs into the Béchamel sauce and pour over the macaroni. Bake for 40–45 minutes until the top is golden-brown.

Serves 6.

Variation

Aubergine pastichio Omit green pepper, mushrooms and courgette, and replace with 1 large chopped aubergine with juices drained.

★ Tip

For a quicker topping, mix together 1 beaten egg and 150 ml/¼ pint natural yoghurt, and top with 25 g/1 oz Cheddar cheese.

TOMATO, FENNEL AND POTATO PIE   F

It is the fennel in this dish that gives a pleasant aroma and delicious aniseed flavour.

8 medium potatoes, washed
1 large bulb of fennel, sliced
6 large tomatoes, sliced
1 small onion, cut into thin rings
75 g/3 oz Cheddar or Gruyère cheese, grated
100 ml/4 fl oz olive or sunflower oil

Pre-heat the oven to 200°C/400°F/ gas 6 and bake the potatoes in their jackets for about 1 hour, until tender. Cool and slice, removing the skins if desired. Blanch the fennel in boiling water for 3 minutes, drain.

Place a layer of potatoes in the base of an ovenproof dish followed by a layer of fennel, tomato and onion, sprinkle with a little cheese. Repeat the layering process, ending with a tomato layer. Pour the oil over the top of the dish and return to the oven for about 20 minutes, until the top is browned.

RATATOUILLE

450 g/1 lb aubergines
450 g/1 lb courgettes
salt
2 × 15 ml spoons/2 tbsp olive oil
2 onions, chopped
2 cloves garlic, crushed
1 red pepper, deseeded and sliced
1 green pepper, deseeded and sliced
200 g/7 oz can chopped tomatoes and juice
freshly ground black pepper
400 g/14 oz can kidney beans, drained (optional)

Cut the aubergines and courgettes into small chunks. Place on a chopping board that has been covered with absorbent paper and generously sprinkle with salt. Top with a second board and leave for 1 hour. This will draw out the bitter taste in the aubergine and reduce the water content of both vegetables. Rinse and pat dry with absorbent paper or a clean tea-towel.

Heat the oil and gently fry the onion until soft and lightly golden. Add the aubergine, courgette, garlic, and peppers, cover and cook gently for 30 minutes. Add the tomatoes to the pan and cook for a further 30 minutes. Season to taste and add the kidney beans, if using. Cook for another 10 minutes, then serve hot; or allow to go cold and serve as a salad.

Variation

Ratatouille crumble Pre-heat oven to 200°C/400°F/gas 6. Rub together 100 g/4 oz wholemeal plain flour and 50 g/2 oz sunflower margarine, then add 1 × 5 ml spoon/1 tsp mixed herbs. Place ratatouille in an ovenproof dish and top with crumble. Cook for 20 minutes.

VEGETABLE PIE   F

The cheese pastry gives this pie added flavour as well as extra protein.

750 g/1½ lb mixed cooked vegetables: potato, carrot, French beans, peas, swede, leek, cabbage
200 g/7 oz can tomatoes, drained
1 × 5 ml spoon/1 tsp yeast extract
1 × 5 ml spoon/1 tsp mixed herbs
salt and freshly ground black pepper
milk, to glaze
1 quantity Cheese Pastry (page 19)

Pre-heat the oven to 200°C/400°F/gas 6.

Turn the cooked vegetables into a 25 cm/10 inch deep pie dish. Chop the tomatoes and mix into the vegetables. Dissolve the yeast extract in 2 × 15 ml spoons/2 tbsp boiling water and pour over the vegetables, sprinkle over the herbs and season to taste.

Roll out the pastry and cut off thin strips long enough to go around the inner rim of the dish. Moisten one side of the strips with a little water and attach to the inside and rim of the dish, then moisten the top side of the pastry strips. Use the remaining pastry to cover the pie dish, pressing it firmly against the pastry strips to seal, and flute the edges. Use the pastry trimmings to make leaves to decorate the top of the pie; moisten one side of the leaves and press that side onto the pastry top. Cut a couple of vents in the top of the pie, brush with a little milk, and bake for 40 minutes, until the pastry is golden-brown and crisp.

SOMETHING SPECIAL

When there is something to celebrate it is easy to think of dishes, such as turkey, salmon, or steak, to serve to meat-eating friends, but thinking of a vegetarian dish worthy of Christmas or a birthday needs a little more imagination. The following dishes, it is hoped, will provide inspiration.

MUSHROOM PLAIT WITH PORT AND CHESTNUT SAUCE   F

The great thing about this Christmas main course is that it can be cooked in advance. It also goes well with the traditional vegetables, and the sauce goes well with turkey.

3 × 15 ml spoons/3 tbsp olive oil
25 g/1 oz butter
4 spring onions, sliced
900 g/2 lb flat mushrooms, chopped
2 cloves of garlic
1 eating apple, peeled and finely chopped
2 × 15 ml spoons/2 tbsp ground almonds
2 × 15 ml spoons/2 tbsp soy sauce
2 × 15 ml spoons/2 tbsp fresh chopped parsley
1 × 5 ml spoon/1 tsp thyme

Pre-heat the oven to 200°C/400°F/ gas 6.

Heat the oil and butter, then add the spring onion, mushrooms, garlic and apple. Cook gently for about 15 minutes, stirring frequently, until all the mushrooms are tender and have given off their liquid. Stir in the almonds, soy sauce, parsley and thyme and cook for a further 5 minutes. Add sufficient breadcrumbs to absorb the cooking liquids without making the mixture dry; season to taste and cool.

75 g/3 oz fresh wholemeal
   breadcrumbs, approx
salt and freshly ground black
   pepper
1½ quantities rich shortcrust
   pastry
egg to glaze

Sauce
40 g/1½ oz butter
1 × 15 ml spoon/1 tbsp very
   finely chopped onion
1 × 15 ml spoon/1 tbsp very
   finely chopped carrot
12 g/½ oz plain flour
100 ml/4 fl oz port
1 bouquet garni
1 bay leaf
225 g/8 oz unsweetened chestnut
   purée
salt and freshly ground black
   pepper

Roll out the pastry on a floured surface to a rectangle 30 × 35 cm/ 12 × 14 inches, moisten the edges with water then make diagonal slits, 7.5 cm/3 inches long and 3 cm/1¼ inches apart, all the way down the two long sides of the pastry. Spread the filling down the centre of the pastry. Fold the cut strips of pastry over the filling to give a plaited effect and seal the edges together carefully down the centre. Fold in the ends and seal well. Chill for at least 30 minutes before cooking.

Brush the pastry with egg to glaze, and bake for 30–35 minutes, until brown. If cooking in advance, under-cook by 5–10 minutes.

For the sauce, melt the butter in a small pan and gently cook the onion and carrot until soft. Sprinkle on the flour and cook for 1 minute, stirring constantly. Gradually add the port, then add the bouquet garni and bay leaf and cook gently until reduced by about one-third. Stir in the chestnut purée and heat through, season to taste and serve hot.

★ Tips

The plait is also good with cranberry and orange sauce.
The mushroom stuffing is excellent in pancakes.

STRAW AND HAY WITH BLACK MUSHROOMS   V F

Dried boletus mushrooms are popular in Italian cooking
for their rich flavour. They are expensive, but fortunately
only a small quantity are needed. These mushrooms are
available in continental delicatessens; alternatively, use
Chinese dried mushrooms. Straw and hay is very fine
pasta that cooks in a couple of minutes. Serve with a
mixed salad and a loaf of crusty Italian-style bread.

25 g/1 oz dried mushrooms
150 ml/¼ pint water
100 g/4 oz flat mushrooms,
  chopped
1 quantity of Tomato Sauce with
  wine (page 17)
4 × 15 ml spoons/4 tbsp
  Parmesan cheese
300 g/10 oz straw and hay
1 × 15 ml spoon/1 tbsp oil

Soak the dried mushrooms in the
water for 30 minutes, drain
reserving the juice. Chop the
dried mushrooms and set aside.
Strain the soaking water through
sieve lined with a sheet of absorbent paper. Follow the instructions
of Tagliatelle with Mushrooms
(page 48), adding both the reserved
water and the chopped dried
mushrooms to the sauce with the
canned tomatoes.

Cook until the sauce is thickened. Meanwhile, cook the straw
and hay in plenty of rapidly
boiling salted water with the oil
added to it until just tender. Drain
and serve with the sauce, sprinkled
with Parmesan cheese (omit for
vegans).

FUSILLI WITH ARTICHOKES

Another quick and easy but delicious dish from Italy. Fusilli (pasta corkscrews) is available in packages containing plain and green varieties, which look especially attractive when cooked.

275 g/10 oz fusilli
1 × 15 ml spoon/1 tbsp oil
75 ml/3 fl oz olive oil
1 large onion, sliced
1 clove of garlic, crushed
400 g/14 oz can artichoke hearts, drained
1 × 15 ml spoon/1 tbsp tomato purée
4 × 15 ml spoons/4 tbsp chopped parsley
50 g/2 oz pine kernels
100 g/4 oz black olives
freshly ground black pepper
4 × 15 ml spoons/4 tbsp Parmesan cheese

Cook the pasta in plenty of rapidly boiling water with the oil added to it for 10–12 minutes, until just tender. Meanwhile, heat the olive oil and cook the onion until soft and clear; add the garlic and cook for another minute. Cut the artichoke hearts into bite-sized pieces and add to the onions with the tomato purée, parsley, pine kernels and olives. Season with pepper and heat through. Drain the pasta and toss with the artichoke mixture, then serve sprinkled with Parmesan cheese.

☆ Microwave tip

Only the sauce is worth making in the microwave. Cook the onion in the oil in a covered dish for 2 minutes on HIGH, add the garlic and cook for 1 minute. Stir in the remaining ingredients, except the Parmesan, and cook for a further 2–3 minutes on HIGH to heat through.

COURGETTE SOUFFLÉ

There is a misplaced fear of cooking soufflés, which are really rather easy. Make sure that you whisk the egg whites well and that you fold them in carefully; don't open the oven door half-way through cooking, and you should be fine.

350 g/12 oz courgettes, topped and tailed
50 g/2 oz butter
50 g/2 oz plain white or wholemeal flour
300 ml/1/2 pint milk
pinch nutmeg
salt and freshly ground black pepper
75 g/3 oz Caerphilly or Wensleydale cheese, grated
4 × 15 ml spoons/4 tbsp chopped parsley
4 eggs, separated

Grease a 1 litre/2 pint soufflé dish thoroughly, tie a collar of lightly greased greaseproof paper around the outside of the dish so that it stands about 5 cm/2 inches above the top of the dish and secure with string. Pre-heat the oven to 190°C/375°F/gas 5.

Cook the courgettes in boiling water until tender. Drain and cool. Chop very finely or place in a food processor (take care not to over-process).

Melt the butter in a pan and stir in the flour, cook for 1 minute, stirring constantly; take off the heat and gradually add the milk. Bring the mixture to the boil, stirring until thickened. Season to taste with nutmeg, salt and pepper. Remove the pan from the heat, beat in the cheese and cool slightly. Beat in the egg yolks, then stir in the courgettes and parsley. Whisk the egg whites until they stand in stiff peaks. Fold about one-third of the egg whites in very thoroughly then fold in the remainder carefully, do not worry if they are not perfectly folded in, this is better than overworking.

Turn the mixture into the soufflé dish. Bake for 30–35 minutes, until well risen and golden-brown.

Variations

Asparagus soufflé Replace the courgettes with 375 g/10 oz package frozen asparagus, cooked until tender.

Cheese and watercress soufflé Increase cheese to 100 g/4 oz, and chop or process ½ bunch watercress leaves and use in place of courgettes.

Spinach soufflé Replace the courgettes with 450 g/1 lb spinach leaves, cooked with only the water clinging to the leaves, until just tender. Drain well and chop finely.

GOUGÈRE WITH PROVENÇAL SAUCE

This dish is made with a ring of cheese-flavoured choux pastry filled with a tomato and aubergine sauce.

50 g/2 oz butter or margarine
150 ml/4 fl oz water
65 g/2½ oz wholemeal flour
2 eggs, beaten
50 g/2 oz Cheddar cheese, grated

Sauce
2 × 15 ml spoons/2 tbsp olive oil
1 onion, chopped
2 cloves of garlic, crushed
1 green pepper, chopped
1 small aubergine, chopped
400 g/14 oz can chopped
  tomatoes
1 × 15 ml spoon/1 tbsp tomato
  purée
1 × 5 ml spoon/1 tsp mixed
  herbs
salt and freshly ground black
  pepper
2 × 15 ml spoons/2 tbsp chopped
  parsley

Pre-heat the oven to 200°C/400°F/gas 6.

To make the gougère, place the butter or margarine in a pan with the water and bring to the boil. Once the butter has melted, remove from the heat and add the flour all at once; beat the mixture until it is smooth and leaves the sides of the pan. Cool slightly, then add the eggs a little at a time, beating well after each addition, until the mixture is glossy; beat in the cheese. Spoon the pastry onto a greased ovenproof pasta or pie plate to form a large ring. Alternatively, the mixture can be piped into a circle.

To make the sauce, cook the onion in the oil over a gentle heat until soft and clear, add the garlic, pepper and aubergine, and cook for another 10 minutes. Stir in the tomatoes, tomato purée and mixed herbs and season to taste. Cook for 15 minutes.

Pour the filling into the centre of the gougère and bake for 40–45 minutes until the pastry is golden-brown. Sprinkle with parsley and serve immediately.

SALADS

Vegetarian eating really comes into its own when it comes to salads. There are endless ways of combining vegetables, beans and grains with a wonderful range of dressings.

The salads in this chapter are divided into main course salads and unusual, wholefood side salads. The side salads can often be combined to create a meal in themselves.

GREEK SALAD WITH BREAD AND CHEESE

The pitta bread in this recipe is toasted until crisp to give the salad a wonderful array of textures.

1 pitta bread
½ iceberg lettuce, shredded
½ red pepper, cut into rings
3 tomatoes, chopped
225 g/8 oz feta cheese, diced
100 g/4 oz black olives
2 × 15 ml spoons/2 tbsp chopped
  parsley
1 × 15 ml spoon/1 tbsp fresh
  chopped mint
4 × 15 ml spoons/4 tbsp olive oil
juice of 1 large lemon
2.5 ml/½ tsp ground cinnamon
salt and freshly ground black
  pepper

Grill the bread until it is dried out and crisp, cool and break into small pieces, set aside. Place the lettuce, red pepper, tomatoes, feta, olives and herbs in a large salad bowl and toss. Combine the oil, lemon juice, cinnamon and salt and pepper to taste in a small jar and shake until well mixed. Pour over the salad and toss. Just before serving, add the crisp bread.

PASTA, BEAN AND VEGETABLE SALAD   V

The variations on this salad are limitless. This salad is
dressed with a basic olive oil dressing, but you may
prefer to toss it in a creamy mayonnaise instead.

450 g/1 lb pasta bows
*1 × 15 ml spoon/1 tbsp vegetable
  oil*
*225 g/8 oz mixed vegetables;
  broccoli or cauliflower florets,
  French beans, carrot or celery
  sticks, thin slices of courgette,
  mangetout*
4 spring onions, sliced
1 red pepper, sliced
200 g/7 oz can kidney beans
200 g/7 oz can butterbeans
lettuce

Dressing
150 ml/¼ pint olive oil
50 ml/2 fl oz white wine vinegar
*2 × 5 ml spoon/2 tsp Dijon
  mustard*
*2 × 15 ml spoons/2 tbsp chopped
  parsley*
*1 × 15 ml spoon/1 tbsp
  poppy-seeds (optional)*
*salt and freshly ground black
  pepper*

Cook the pasta bows in boiling
water with the oil added until just
tender. Drain and rinse under
cold water to cool, set aside to
drain thoroughly. Place the mixed
vegetables in boiling water and
blanch for 3 minutes, drain and
allow to cool.

Place all the dressing ingredients
in a screw-top jar and shake until
well mixed. Combine the cooled
pasta vegetables, spring onions,
red pepper, kidney beans and
butter beans. Pour over the
dressing and toss. Place on a bed
of lettuce to serve.

RISOTTO SALAD   V

This Italian main course is delicious served cold with a
French dressing.

*2 × 15 ml spoons/ 2 tbsp
  sunflower oil*

Heat the oil in a large saucepan
and fry the onion gently until soft

1 onion, chopped
1 clove of garlic, crushed
225 g/8 oz long-grain brown rice
600 ml/1 pint vegetable stock
1 × 5 ml spoon/1 tsp oregano
salt and freshly ground black
  pepper
200 g/7 oz can sweetcorn
1/2 greeen pepper
1/2 red pepper
1 courgette, sliced
3 small tomatoes, quartered

Dressing
2 × 15 ml spoons/2 tbsp lemon
  juice
75 ml/3 fl oz olive oil
salt and freshly ground black
  pepper

and clear. Add the garlic and the rice and fry for 2 minutes, stirring constantly. Pour in the stock, and add the oregano and seasoning to taste. Cover the pan and simmer for about 30 minutes until the rice is tender. Stir in the sweetcorn, peppers and courgette and transfer to a bowl. Combine the dressing ingredients, pour over the hot risotto and toss. Once cool, add the tomatoes.

Variation

Pepper risotto boats Cut red and yellow peppers in half lengthwise, deseed and fill with risotto. In place of peppers in the risotto use 100 g/4 oz cooked peas.

MIXED SALAD   V

This is the classic side salad which goes well with almost every meal.

1 head radicchio, washed
1/2 head green lettuce, washed
50 g/2 oz French beans, cooked
  and cut into small lengths
2 beefsteak tomatoes, chopped
10 cm/4 inch piece cucumber,
  chopped
1–2 × 15 ml spoons/1–2 tbsp
  olive oil

Break the radicchio and lettuce into leaves, wash, and dry on a clean tea-towel. Mix together the radicchio, lettuce, beans, tomatoes and cucumber in a large bowl, then sprinkle with salt and pepper. Drizzle over the olive oil to taste, toss and serve.

SWEET AND SOUR ORIENTAL SALAD V

This salad has an unusual sweet and sour dressing.

*1 small head Chinese leaves,
shredded*
*200 g/7 oz can water chestnuts,
sliced*
100 g/4 oz bean sprouts

Dressing
3 cloves of garlic, crushed
*2 × 15 ml spoons/2 tbsp soy
sauce*
*1 × 5 ml spoon/1 tsp red wine
vinegar*
*1 × 5 ml spoon/1 tsp Tabasco
sauce*
1 × 5 ml spoon/1 tsp salt
*1 × 15 ml spoon/1 tbsp caster
sugar*

Mix together all the ingredients for the dressing until the sugar has dissolved. Taste and add more salt and sugar, if required. Place the shredded Chinese leaves in a bowl, pour over the dressing and toss. Leave to stand for at least one hour. About 5 minutes before serving, add the water chestnuts and bean sprouts to the bowl and toss to combine.

★ Tip

Other vegetables that could be added to this salad include: thinly sliced carrots and courgettes, sliced spring onions, sliced red pepper, bamboo shoots and sliced mushrooms. To add protein, include fried bean-curd cubes or toasted almonds or cashew nuts.

SPICED BEAN SALAD   V

Choose a selection of beans of your choice, but try to keep your selection colourful. You can use canned beans if your are in a hurry.

675 g/1½ lb beans, soaked overnight: haricot, borlotti, flageolets, red kidney, Dutch brown, black-eye, butter or chick-peas or black beans

Dressing
1 small onion, grated
1 dried red chilli pepper, crumbled
150 ml/¼ pint olive oil
juice of 3 lemons
salt and freshly ground black pepper

Discard the water the beans have been soaking in and cover with fresh water. Boil rapidly for at least 10 minutes then simmer for 1½–2 hours, until all the beans are tender. Rinse in cold water, drain and leave to cool. Mix all the ingredients for the dressing together, pour over the beans and toss lightly as some of the beans will be very soft and may break up if not handled gently. If using canned beans, simply drain well and toss with the dressing.

DATE, APPLE AND WALNUT SALAD

2 red eating apples, cored and sliced
juice of ½ lemon
100 g/4 oz dates, stoned and sliced
50 g/2 oz walnuts
2 sticks celery
4 × 15 ml spoons/4 tbsp mayonnaise
4 × 15 ml spoons/4 tbsp natural yoghurt
shredded lettuce (optional)

Toss the apples in lemon juice then combine with the dates, walnuts and celery. Mix together the mayonnaise and yoghurt and spoon over the salad, then stir gently until evenly coated. Serve on a bed of shredded lettuce, if desired.

Variation

Waldorf salad Leave out the dates, use 6 sticks of celery and 150 ml/¼ pint mayonnaise without yoghurt.

UNUSUAL ACCOMPANIMENTS

A side dish of delicious vegetables really delights the vegetarian. So often vegetables are served plain, maybe with just a knob of butter or with a plain white sauce. Here are some much more interesting ideas that will perk up even the dullest vegetables. Try reducing the salt content of your vegetables to let the natural flavours come through, and reduce the cooking time so that they still have a bit of bite left in them. As a bonus, you will have boiled away fewer of the nutrients.

STUFFED SPANISH ONIONS

When onions are cooked slowly they develop a creamy sweetness which is quite distinct from the harshness of the raw vegetable.

4 Spanish onions
2 mushrooms
1 large tomato, skinned
100 g/4 oz breadcrumbs
1 × 5 ml spoon/1 tsp mixed
  herbs
salt and freshly ground black
  pepper
25 g/1 oz Cheddar cheese

Pre-heat the oven to 200°C/400°F/ gas 6.

Trim the roots from the onions and peel off the other skin. Add to a pan of boiling water, cover and simmer for 1 hour. Remove from the pan, reserving 4 × 15 ml spoons/4 tbsp cooking water, and allow the onions to cool slightly. Carefully remove the inner parts of the onion, leaving two or three outer layers intact and place in a food processor with the mushroom, tomato, all but 2 × 15 ml spoons/2 tbsp breadcrumbs, herbs and seasoning to taste, blend until a fine mixture is obtained. Stuff back into the centre of the onions. Combine the remaining breadcrumbs and cheese and sprinkle over the top of the onions.

Place the onions in an ovenproof dish, pour around the reserved cooking liquid and cover with foil. Bake for about 25 minutes. Remove the cover and cook for a further 5 minutes, or until the tops are golden-brown.

CRISPY ONION RINGS

A very popular vegetable which goes well with potato-topped pie dishes.

4 large onions, cut into slices
75 ml/3 fl oz milk
50 g/2 oz plain wholemeal flour
salt and freshly ground black
  pepper
oil for deep frying
paprika

Separate the onion slices into rings. Place the flour on a plate and season with salt and pepper. Dip the onion rings into the milk, then dip in the flour. Fry a few rings at a time in hot oil for 2–3 minutes until golden-brown, drain on absorbent paper and keep warm.

OKRA WITH TOMATOES   F V

Okra, otherwise known as Lady's Fingers, is a small, pod-shaped vegetable with a slightly aromatic flavour. It originally came from the West Indies, but is now grown in other parts of the world and is available all the year round. When buying, choose young small pods that are a fresh green colour and avoid any that are yellowing or limp.

450 g/1 lb okra
2 × 15 ml spoons/2 tbsp
  sunflower oil
1 onion, sliced
2 cloves of garlic, crushed
400 g/1 lb can chopped tomatoes
salt and freshly ground black
  pepper
juice 1 lemon

Wash the okra and wipe off any hair using absorbent paper. Carefully trim off the stems, but do not cut into the okra itself as it releases a sticky fluid when cooking. Heat the oil and gently fry the onion until lightly golden, add the garlic and cook for 1 minute. Add the okra, tomatoes, seasoning and lemon juice and stir well. Bring to the boil, cover and cook for about 40 minutes, stir occasionally taking care not to damage the okra. When the okra is tender serve hot or cold as a salad.

Variation

Curried okra and tomatoes To turn this into an Indian dish, when adding the garlic, stir in 1 × 5 ml spoon/1 tsp each of ground turmeric, ground coriander and cumin seeds, and add 1 × 5 ml spoon/1 tsp sugar with the lemon juice.

GRATED COURGETTES IN ORANGE

This is a delicious way to serve courgettes. They can be cooked in the same way but using lemon juice too.

3 courgettes, trimmed
juice and rind of ½ orange
25 g/1 oz butter
salt and freshly ground black
  pepper

Coarsely grate the courgettes into a bowl with a steel grater. Add the orange rind and juice and leave for at least one hour. Heat the butter in a wok or frying-pan and add the courgettes. Stir-fry for 2–3 minutes until tender, then season to taste.

RED CABBAGE WITH APPLE AND WALNUTS   F V

This dish is a fabulour colour and would cheer up a dull plate. The added protein in the walnuts is useful if you feel your main course was low in this department.

625 g/1½ lb red cabbage,
  shredded
2 large cooking apples, peeled,
  cored and chopped
1 large onion, sliced
50 g/2 oz walnut pieces
50 g/2 oz raisins
1 × 15 ml spoon/1 tbsp brown
  sugar
1 × 5 ml spoon/1 tsp salt
3 × 15 ml spoons/3 tbsp red
  wine vinegar
2.5 ml/½ tsp dry mustard
150 ml/¼ pint apple juice

Pre-heat the oven to 170°C/325°F/ gas 3.

   Mix all the ingredients in a casserole dish. Cover tightly and cook for 1½–2 hours, stirring occasionally until the cabbage is tender.

SESAME CARROTS WITH CHIVES

450 g/1 lb small carrots
50 g/2 oz butter
*2 × 15 ml spoons/2 tbsp sesame
   seeds*
*1 × 15 ml spoon/1 tbsp snipped
   fresh chives*
*salt and freshly ground black
   pepper*

Leave tiny carrots whole, slice larger ones in half lengthwise. Boil in slightly salted water until just tender, drain.

Meanwhile, melt the butter. Pour over the carrots and shake gently. Sprinkle over the sesame seeds, chives and seasoning to taste and toss to coat evenly.

☆ <u>Microwave tip</u>

Cook carrots or French beans in 4 × 15 ml spoons/4 tbsp water for about 8 minutes on HIGH, leave to stand for 5 minutes. Melt the butter on HIGH for 1 minute.

FRENCH BEANS IN CREAMY MUSTARD SAUCE

This is a cheat's sauce made in minutes. It is also good with broad beans, carrots or turnips.

*450 g/1 lb French beans,
   trimmed*
*4 × 15 ml spoons/4 tbsp
   mayonnaise*
*3 × 15 ml spoons/3 tbsp milk or
   natural yoghurt*
*1 × 5 ml spoon/1 tsp Dijon
   mustard*
1 × 5 ml spoon/1 tsp tarragon

Cook the beans in slightly salted water until tender, drain. Meanwhile, mix together the sauce ingredients in a small pan and heat through without boiling. Pour the sauce over the beans and serve.

CELERIAC AND CARROT MATCHSTICKS

Celeriac is becoming easier to find now. It tastes like nutty celery while it is treated more like a turnip. Here the combination of orange and white looks and tastes impressive.

225 g/8 oz celeriac, cut into matchsticks
225 g/8 oz carrots, cut into matchsticks
50 g/2 oz butter or margarine
garlic salt and freshly ground black pepper
2 × 15 ml spoons/2 tbsp fresh chopped parsley

Blanch the vegetables in slightly salted water for 2 minutes. Heat the butter or margarine in a pan and cook the vegetables over a gentle heat until just tender. Season with garlic salt and toss in the parsley.

CANDIED SWEET POTATOES

This dish comes from the southern states of America, where it is popular with pork dishes. It tastes good with vegetarian dishes such as cheese and onion pie, or with a courgette soufflé.

450 g/1 lb sweet potatoes, peeled and sliced
3 × 15 ml spoons/3 tbsp brown sugar
1 × 15 ml spoons/1 tbsp orange juice
grated rind of 1 orange
2 × 15 ml spoons/2 tbsp hot water
generous pinch ground ginger
25 g/1 oz butter

Pre-heat the oven to 180°C/350°F/gas 4.

Parboil the sweet potatoes for 5 minutes, drain and place in a buttered casserole dish. Meanwhile, combine the sugar, orange juice and rind, water, ginger and butter in a small saucepan, heat gently until the sugar has dissolved. Pour over the sweet potatoes and bake for 25–30 minutes until the sweet potatoes are tender. Baste the sweet potatoes in the syrup occasionally whilst cooking.

SWEET AND FANCIFUL

Vegetarians can eat almost all desserts and cakes with the exception of those made with gelatine and suet. However, careful planning is needed when choosing a dessert. For instance, if a main course has relied on dairy products for its protein, do not serve a cheesecake. On the other hand, if the main course has been light on protein, a dessert based on eggs and milk may be nutritionally valuable.

HONEY AND LEMON CAKE   F

200 ml/7 fl oz clear honey
25 g/1 oz butter or margarine
175 g/7 oz wholemeal
    self-raising flour
pinch salt
1 ×5 ml spoon/1 tsp mixed spice
grated rind of 1 large lemon
juice of 1½ lemons
1 egg, beaten
50 g/2 oz light brown sugar

Pre-heat the oven to 180°C/350°F/gas 4.

Grease and line the base of a 20 cm/8 inch round tin. Heat together the honey and butter or margarine until melted. Remove from the heat and stir in the flour, salt, spice and lemon rind, egg and 3 × 15 ml spoons/3 tbsp lemon juice. Turn the mixture into the tin and bake for 30–40 minutes until golden-brown and a cocktail stick inserted into the centre comes out clean.

Turn out onto a wire rack and while still hot, combine the remaining lemon juice and sugar and spoon over the cake top. Leave to cool.

BAKEWELL TART

Serve warm with single cream as a dessert or cold at tea time.

1 quantity shortcrust pastry (page 19)
100 g/4 oz soft margarine or butter
100 g/4 oz light brown sugar
2 eggs, beaten
few drops almond essence
25 g/1 oz plain wholemeal flour
50 g/2 oz ground almonds
3 × 15 ml spoons/3 tbsp raspberry or plum jam

Pre-heat the oven to 200°C/400°F/gas 6.

Roll out the pastry on a floured surface and use to line a greased 18 cm/7 inch greased flan dish. Chill while making filling but retain leftover pastry. Cream together the butter or margarine and sugar until light and fluffy, then gradually beat in the eggs and flavour with a few drops of almond essence. Fold in the flour and ground almonds.

Spread the jam over the pastry base, and spread the almond mixture over it. Roll the remaining pastry and cut out strips 19 × 1 cm/7½ × ½ inches. Lay over the flan in a criss-cross pattern and secure the ends to the pastry crust with a little water. Glaze the pastry with milk and bake at the high setting for 5 minutes, the reduce the heat to 180°C/350°F/gas 4 and bake for a further 30 minutes, until golden and firm.

GRAPE JELLY

This recipe uses agar agar, which is available in health food shops, to set the jelly.

600 ml/1 pint red grape juice
1 × 15 ml spoons/1 tbsp agar
  agar (or follow package direc-
  tions)
2 × 15 ml spoons/2 tbsp
  Cointreau (optional)
1 × 5 ml spoon/1 tsp lemon juice
100 g/4 oz black grapes, pips
  removed and halved
blanched almonds

Bring 150 ml/¼ pint of the grape juice to the boil, sprinkle over the agar agar and stir until dissolved, which takes at least 5 minutes. Remove from the heat. Place the hot liquid in a bowl, add the remaining grape juice and stir in the Cointreau, if using, and the lemon juice. Allow to cool until half set. Divide the grapes between four glass dishes and pour over the half-set jelly. Garnish with blanched almonds.

BLINTZES

Dessert pancakes fill up a hole at the end of a light meal.

1 quantity pancakes (page 18)
350 g/12 oz ricotta or low-fat
  cream cheese
150 ml/¼ pint natural yoghurt
50 g/2 oz sultanas
1 × 5 ml spoon/1 tsp vanilla
  flavouring
1 × 15 ml/1 tbsp clear honey

Pre-heat the oven to 180°C/350°F/ gas 4.
  Make the pancakes as directed. Beat together the cheese and 2 × 15 ml spoons/2 tbsp yoghurt until smooth, then mix in the remaining ingredients. Fill the pancakes by folding each pancake in half and then in half again and placing the mixture in the result-ing cone. Place the pancakes in an ovenproof dish, cover with foil and cook for 15–20 minutes, until the pancakes are warmed through.

CANTALOUPE SORBET

1 large cantaloupe melon
150 ml/½ pint water
1–2 × 15 ml spoons/1–2 tbsp
 clear honey
2 egg whites, whisked

Cut the melon in half and remove the seeds. Scoop all of the flesh off the skin and place in a blender with the water and honey to taste. Blend until smooth. Transfer the mixture to a shallow freezer tray and freeze until almost frozen. Mash into a pulp, then fold in the whisked egg whites. Return to the freezer, and leave to freeze completely.

To serve, remove from the freezer about 15 minutes prior to serving to soften slightly. Scoop into bowls to serve.

MINCEMEAT

Vegetarian mincemeat, without the suet, is every bit as flavoursome as its original – but lower in fat. It does not keep so well, so if you are not going to use it all at once, freeze in a plastic container.

350 g/12 oz mixed fruit
2 eating apples, peeled, cored
 and very finely chopped
25 g/1 oz dried apricots, very
 finely chopped
25 g/1 oz chopped almonds
2 × 5 ml spoon/2 tsp mixed spice
1 × 5 ml spoon/1 tsp ground
 cinnamon
2 × 5 ml spoon/2 tsp clear
 honey
grated rind and juice of 1 orange
2 × 15 ml spoons/2 tbsp brandy

Combine all of the ingredients together, adjusting the sweetness and spiciness by adding a little more honey and spices, if desired. (You may wish to chop the fruit in a food processor; if so, also chop half of the dried fruit for a finer textured mincemeat.) If the mixture looks too dry, add a little more orange juice. Place in jars previously sterilized in boiling water and dried in a low oven.

Makes 625 g/1½ lb.

MINCE PIES

1 quantity Orange Pastry
   (page 19)
350 g/12 oz mincemeat
1 egg, beaten
sifted icing sugar, to serve

Pre-heat the oven to 200°C/400°F/gas 6.

Roll out the pastry quite thinly on a floured surface, and using large and medium fluted cutters, cut out as many bases and tops from the pastry as possible. You should make about 18 of each. Gently press the large pastry discs into greased patty tins and place a heaped teaspoonful of mincemeat into each, do not overfill. Moisten the edges of the pastry with a little water and press a small lid on top of each pie, sealing well. Prick each pie with a fork to let out the steam and brush with beaten egg.

Bake the mince pies for about 12 minutes until the pastry is golden, transfer to a wire rack to cool. Serve warm or cold dusted with sifted icing sugar.

★ Tip

Orange pastry must be chilled for 30 minutes before using as it is very short. If you take a long time in making your mince pies, chill them again for 15–30 minutes before cooking.

CHERRY-TOPPED CHEESECAKE F

Cheesecakes are full of eggs and cheese which can add protein to a vegetable-based meal – they also add dairy fats, so be sure not to serve with a main course which is also high in fats.

Base
120 g/4 oz butter or margarine
225 g/8 oz digestive biscuits crumbled

Filling
450g/1 lb low fat cream cheese
175 g/6 oz caster sugar
2 × 15 ml spoon/2 tbsp lemon juice
40 g/1½ oz flour
generous pinch of salt
1 × 5 ml spoon/1 tsp vanilla essence
3 eggs, separated
175 ml/6 fl oz double cream or cream substitute

Topping
325 g/11 oz can stoned black cherries
clear honey (optional)

Pre-heat the oven to 150°C/300°F/gas 2.

Grease and line the base of a 23 cm/9 inch loose-bottomed tin. Melt the butter and mix into the biscuit crumbs, then firmly press into the base of the tin. Chill while making filling.

Combine the cheese, 100 g/4 oz of the sugar, lemon juice, flour, salt and vanilla essence. Whisk the egg yolks and beat into the cheese mixture. Whip the cream until stiff and fold in carefully. Whip the egg whites until stiff, fold in the remaining sugar and whip until glossy, then gently fold in. Spoon the cheesecake mixture over the base and bake for 1¼ hours. Leave in the cooling oven until cold.

Strain the cherries, reserving the juice, place in a blender and purée until smooth. Add honey to taste, if required, and add a little cherry juice if the purée is too thick. Spread the topping over the cheesecake and chill.

NO-EGG FRUIT CAKE   F V

A reduced fat cake that is not lacking flavour. Choose sunflower margarine if making the cake for vegans, and remember that most marzipans and icings contain eggs, so it's best to leave the cake plain.

175 g/6 oz butter or sunflower margarine
225 g/8 oz muscavado sugar
450 g/1 lb plain wholemeal flour
2.5 ml/½ tsp cinnamon
2.5 ml/½ tsp mixed spice
175 g/6 oz raisins
100 g/4 oz sultanas
50 g/2 oz glacé cherries, chopped
3 × 15 ml spoons/3 tbsp vinegar
175 ml/6 fl oz skimmed milk
2 × 5 ml spoons/2 tsp bicarbonate of soda

Pre-heat the oven to 160°C/325°F/gas 3.

Line a 20 cm/8 inch round tin with two layers of greaseproof paper and oil well, dust lightly with white flour.

Cream together the butter or margarine and sugar until fluffy, then fold in the flour and spices followed by the fruit. Combine the vinegar and milk in a large bowl and add the bicarbonate of soda – this mixture will curdle slightly then froth. Stir at once into the cake mixture. Turn into the prepared tin and bake for 1½ hours or until a skewer inserted into the centre comes out clean.

★ Tips

If you do wish to use eggs, beat together 3 eggs and beat into the creamed fat and sugar adding a little flour if the mixture looks like curdling use only 2·5 × 5 ml spoon – ½ tsp.

Glacé cherries are now available that use natural not synthetic red dyes. They are a darker, less artificial colour and can be found in health food shops and large supermarkets.

MENUS

Sunday lunch for vegetarians and non-vegetarians

Gazpacho	25
Roast Lamb	
Vegetable Cheese Surprise	45
Roast Potatoes	
Grape Jelly with Ice Cream	88

Vegan meal

Chick-pea Soup	22
Budget Vegetable Hotpot	61
Mixed Salad	77

Christmas dinner

Cream of Celery Soup	22
Mushroom Plait with Port and Chestnut Sauce	68
Carrots	
Brussels Sprouts	
Roast Potatoes	
Mince Pies with Brandy Butter	90

Special occasion dinner

Almond, Potato and Watercress Soup	24
French Bread and Butter	
Gougère	74
Mixed Salad	77
Cantaloupe Sorbet	89

INDEX OF RECIPES

THE FAMILY MATTERS SERIES